AMERICA'S HOUSING CRISIS

BERTHA DAVIS

AMERICA'S HOUSING CRISIS

Franklin Watts
New York London Toronto Sydney
An Impact Book 1990

Diagrams by Vantage Art, Inc.

Photographs courtesy of:
Bettmann Archive: pp. 17 top, 64; Impact Visuals:
pp. 17 bottom (Donna Binder), 27 top (Kirk Condyles),
27 bottom (Amy Zuckerman), 67 top (Cindy Reiman),
124 top (Cindy Reiman); AP/ Wide World: pp. 36,
39, 57, 67 bottom, 102, 110, 120, 124 bottom; Photo
Researchers: pp. 82 top, 112 (Bettye Lane); Black
Star: p. 82 bottom; UPI: p. 97.

Library of Congress Cataloging-in-Publication Data
Davis, Bertha, 1910–
America's housing crisis / Bertha Davis.
p.   cm. — (An Impact book)
Includes bibliographical references (p.   )
Summary: Surveys the topic of housing in modern America,
examining such aspects as the low-income rental housing crisis,
public housing, and the question of renting versus buying a home.
ISBN 0-531-10917-8
1. Housing—United States—Juvenile literature.   2. Housing
policy—United States—Juvenile literature.   3. Housing subsidies
—United States—Juvenile literature.   [Housing.]   I. Title.
HD7293.D315   1990
363.5′0973—dc20   89-37028   CIP   AC

BOOKS BY BERTHA DAVIS

Crisis in Industry:
Can America Compete?

The National Debt

Instead of Prison

CONTENTS

Foreword

11

Chapter One
Homelessness: A Symptom

13

Chapter Two
The Low-Income
Rental Housing Crisis.

21

Chapter Three
The World of Public Housing

31

Chapter Four
The Voucher Idea

45

Chapter Five
Renters on Their Own

59

Chapter Six
The Plight of the Would-Be Home Buyer
71

Chapter Seven
Low-Income Housing? Of Course!
But Not Here
89

Chapter Eight
For Rent/For Sale—But Only
to the ''Right'' People
99

Chapter Nine
Housing's Thousand Points of Light
115

——

Source Notes 131
Glossary 135
Suggested Reading List 139
Index 141

A WORD ABOUT NAMES

When names like *Josephine C.* or *William C.* are used, that is, a first name and a surname initial, the individuals named are real people whose stories appeared in newspapers or other printed material. People identified simply as *Annie* or *the Does* are fictitious, but they are true to life.

FOREWORD

SOMEWHERE in the United States, no one knows exactly where, there is a house or apartment that should have on its door a plaque that reads:

This house (or apartment), completed in 1987, brings the number of housing units in the United States to a grand total of 100,000,000.

The creation of over one hundred million places to live—the vast majority of them acceptable places to live—is a remarkable achievement, and the 1982 President's Commission on Housing cannot be faulted for assuring the nation that "Americans today are the best-housed people in history."

But the Housing Act of 1949 set the goal of "a decent home and suitable living environment" not just for most American families but "for every American family." That goal has not been achieved. Right now, in fact, we are losing ground rather than moving ahead on the housing front.

The scandals involving the federal Department of Housing and Urban Development that have been front-page news for the past several months make clear that the nation does not always receive full value for money spent to achieve housing goals. But fraud and mismanagement within the housing bureaucracy, the pursuit of private gain rather than public purpose in the private sector—distressing as they are—do not explain America's current housing crisis.

What are the real signals of that crisis? What are the authentic signs of retreat rather than progress on the housing front? Why are they happening? These questions are the focus of this book.

CHAPTER ONE

HOMELESSNESS: A SYMPTOM

Josephine C. closed the door behind herself and her five children for the last time on December 27, 1983. Behind her she left a one-family house on a leafy street in Cambria Heights in southeastern Queens. Once the property of her common-law husband, they had lived in the home for ten years until they separated and the bank foreclosed on a mortgage she could no longer pay. A local speculator bought it and asked for $350 rent. This was almost a hundred dollars more than the amount she received in her welfare check for shelter. She was soon evicted.

As she and her children came down the stoop they stepped across this city's sharpest dividing line between haves and have-nots, between the merely poor and the desperate. They stepped out of one world and into another. They were now homeless.[1]

As RECENTLY as ten years ago nobody talked of a "homelessness crisis." That phrase emerged in the 1980s as the ranks of people with no place to call home burgeoned dramatically in numbers and diversity.

GETTING A FIX
ON THE NUMBERS

For obvious reasons the homeless are difficult to count. A 1983 report by the Department of Housing and Urban Development (HUD) estimated a national homeless population of between 250,000 and 350,000.[2] In contrast, the Coalition for the Homeless and the Committee for Creative Non-Violence, two advocacy groups for the homeless, have offered estimates of between two and three million.[3]

A firmer figure may soon be available. In 1990 the Census Bureau embarks upon the constitutionally mandated decennial census, and its plans include a special effort directed toward the homeless. On March 20, 1990, between 6:00 P.M. and midnight, census takers will go to public and private shelters for the homeless to record the individuals and families being cared for. "Where people are sleeping, we won't awaken them. We'll just try to estimate their age, sex and things like that," a census official promised. Then, between 2:00 and 4:00 A.M. they will cover street locations where the homeless are known to gather.

While there is general agreement that "How many homeless are there?" is an important question, many go along with the point of view voiced by Minnesota Congressman Bruce F. Vento that we "shouldn't be diverted by an argument about numbers. The obvious fact is that we have a growing number of homeless."

THE CHANGING FACE OF HOMELESSNESS

The homeless of yesterday were predominantly elderly white males, generally labeled "vagrants" or "tramps" or "skid row bums." In contrast, the diversity of today's homeless is as disturbing as their growing numbers. One large group—generally agreed to be at least one-third of the total—are mentally ill individuals. Another third is made up of single men, generally younger than in earlier years, many the victims of drug or alcohol addiction, many with criminal histories.[4]

The changing faces of homelessness: (Top) In 1886 male vagrants paid five cents a night for a floor to sleep on and a roof over their heads. (Bottom) In 1987 a mother and daughter seek refuge in a Brooklyn shelter.

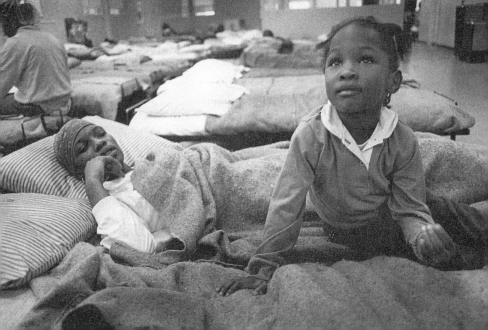

The fastest-growing group, already estimated at nearly one-third of the total, is made up of families. In some big cities that percentage is substantially larger. Estimates from the U.S. Conference of Mayors indicate that in 1986 families with children made up 40 percent of the homeless in Chicago and Boston, 66 percent in New York City, and 80 percent in Yonkers, New York. A later estimate of family structure, from the same source, suggested that 30 percent of homeless families are headed by two parents.[5]

When one asks why this family or that family became homeless, about one-third of the time one learns that something had happened to the family's home. More often than not, fire had destroyed it. But perhaps an order to vacate a building had come because the boiler of the heating system had burst or a major plumbing connection had sprung a leak and cut off the water supply.

Well over two-thirds of the time, however, the family is homeless because it was evicted for nonpayment of rent. But not all homeless families are totally without income. The 1983 HUD study concluded that about 20 to 25 percent of the homeless are employed, mostly in part-time or temporary jobs. Another 30 to 35 percent were found to be receiving some form of public assistance under federal or local welfare programs.[6] But what comes in, for families that become homeless, just doesn't cover the amounts that have to go out. As Sister Connie Driscoll says of many of the women who arrive at her Chicago shelter: "They have a choice to make. Pay the rent or eat." Some families choose to eat.

THE NEAR HOMELESS— DOUBLING UP

One out-of-town observer of New York City's homeless scene commented wonderingly: "I can't imagine that they don't have anybody—a sister or cousin or aunt—who would take them in until they get on their feet." Many do have, of course. The National Coalition for the Homeless estimated at the end of 1985 that there were as many as 3 to 6 million families doubling up.[7] They cling to that resource for as long as they can. But when displaced families double up with families or friends, the tensions that these arrangements create often produce a predictable outcome. Many shelters report that among the high percentage of families that seek shelter because they were evicted, over half were "evictions" from homes of relatives or friends.

THE ONE COMMON CAUSE
OF HOMELESSNESS

Simply naming the major groups of the homeless acknowledges the complex web of causes that contribute to the problem. It makes painfully clear the range of remedies and services required to deal with those causes. Nonetheless, consensus on two points prevails among informed activists involved with the homeless: (1) Regardless of the cause of their other problems, the cause of their homelessness is a shortage of low-income housing that has reached crisis proportions; (2) the rising tide of homelessness will not turn unless the low-income housing crisis changes for the better.

The indicators of a low-income housing crisis are unmistakable. One is that the demand for such housing far exceeds the supply. A 1986 state-by-state survey by the National Low-Income Housing Coalition compared the number of households needing low-cost housing in a given state with the number of low-cost housing units available in that state. The study showed that in most states the number of needed units was two, three, even four times greater than the number of available units.[8]

Another indicator is that rents for low-cost housing have gone up so much more sharply than incomes in recent years that a growing percentage of families must spend far more than they can afford for shelter. They have nothing to fall back upon if illness strikes or the wage earner loses his or her job.

OTHER HOUSING PROBLEMS

Homelessness, then, is a symptom, a symptom of the low-income housing crisis that plagues our nation. But that is not our only housing problem. As New York's Governor Mario Cuomo reminds us: "Unfortunately, the homeless are only the most visible victims of a housing crisis that affects Americans at virtually every economic level." In other words, in addition to a shortage of low-income housing that has reached crisis proportions, there are other housing problems that surfaced in the 1980s or persisted from earlier days. Some of them are:

- a rental market in which thousands of middle-class Americans look in vain for available, affordable units that meet their needs
- a decline in home ownership
- despite enormous progress in improving the physical condition of the nation's housing, the continued presence in the housing stock of millions of substandard units
- the persistence of housing discrimination based on income, race, and family structure

These days the poor are not the only ones with housing problems. But we start with them.

CHAPTER TWO

THE LOW-INCOME RENTAL HOUSING CRISIS

While Annie was living with her three children on the twelfth floor of the Martinique Hotel (a hotel formerly used by New York City to house homeless families) she was told by her social worker that she must demonstrate that she was trying to find an apartment. "Your rent allowance," the social worker reminded her, "is $286 a month." Every newspaper Annie looked at and every real estate office she visited told her that there were no available apartments at that price.

WHY WAS Annie's need to find an apartment for her family in the mid-1980s far more hopeless than it would have been ten years earlier? Why, in other words, has the shortage of rental housing for poor households taken on the dimensions of a crisis in recent years?

The answer lies in two unpleasant facts: (1) The number of poor households continues to be high. (2) The number of housing units affordable to poor households has gone down.

THE PERSISTENCE OF POVERTY

"The number of poor households continues to be high." That fact requires some definitions. What is a "household"? What does "poor" mean? According to the Census Bureau, the government agency that collects and organizes population facts, a *household* is one or more people occupying a housing unit. As of March 1988 there were 91.1 million households in the United States. A *family* includes at least two people related through birth, adoption, or marriage. As of March 1988, 65.1 million of the 91.1 million households were families.[1] (This book will use the two terms interchangeably.)

Poor—for statistical purposes—means having an income below the poverty level. The Poverty Statistics Office of the Census Bureau's Housing Division computes poverty levels for families of varying size and composition and for individuals. For example, as of September 1988 the poverty level for a family of four was $11,600. That figure means that at that time four people needed an income of $11,600 to maintain an adequate diet and meet their other basic needs. An income below that level would force the family to do without some necessities. They would be, technically, poor.

As the figures on page 25 show, the poverty level income for an individual living alone and the levels for a family of two, or six, or nine are different from that of a family of four. The family-of-four figure is the one most frequently cited in the media.

Individuals and families whose incomes put them below their poverty levels are poor. And their numbers are not going down. In 1986, there were 32.4 million Americans (13.6 percent of the population) below the poverty level; in 1987, 32.5 million (13.5 percent of the population) were below that level.[2]

Everybody who is poor is not poor enough to be considered eligible for housing assistance, according to HUD's standards. To identify that group, some additional terms must be defined. Income levels vary widely from place to place in the United States and those differences must be taken into consideration in administering government programs. For housing assistance purposes the country is divided into areas and the *median family income* for each of those areas is computed by HUD. If the median income in Area X is $15,000, that means that half the households in Area X have incomes above $15,000 and half have incomes below that amount.

POVERTY THRESHOLDS IN 1987

Size of Family Unit	Threshold
One person (unrelated individual)	$ 5,778
15 to 64 years	5,909
65 years and over	5,447
Two persons	7,397
Householder 15 to 64 years	7,641
Householder 65 years and over	6,872
Three persons	9,056
Four persons	11,611
Five persons	13,737
Six persons	15,509
Seven persons	17,649
Eight persons	19,515
Nine persons or more	23,105

Source: *Money Income and Poverty Status in the United States: 1987.* U.S. Department of Commerce, Current Population Reports, Bureau of the Census: Series P-60, No. 161, August 1988, p. 41.

Households whose incomes are between 50 and 80 percent of the median are classified as *lower income* families; those whose incomes are below 50 percent of the median are classified as *low-income* families. These two groups are the only ones considered eligible for most kinds of housing assistance.

THE DECLINING SUPPLY OF LOW-INCOME HOUSING

Why has the supply of housing affordable to low-income renters gone down? *Gentrification* is one reason.

For many years the private housing market met, to a degree, the needs of low-income renters through a process called *filtering,* that worked like this. Upwardly mobile families would buy newly constructed housing, larger perhaps or more luxurious than their present quarters. The housing they left behind when they moved to their new homes then became available to other families able to make a move up from less desirable housing. These families' moves made *their* housing available to families ready for a move up from even less desirable housing, and what *they* left was housing likely to be affordable to families pretty far down on the income scale.

In recent years, filtering has gone into reverse in many areas. For a variety of reasons, older, urban housing that once would have become available to low-income households has been snatched up by affluent buyers who proceed to modernize and face-lift the property. Whole neighborhoods have been transformed as this process of *gentrification* goes on. As a result, substantial numbers of housing units drop out of the low-cost housing supply.

Then there was urban renewal, a good idea that had a devastating impact on low-income housing. In the 1950s and 1960s, many of the nation's large cities faced serious problems as thousands of their residents joined the surge to the suburbs. Downtown business districts were lined with closed shops and half-empty office buildings. Because it was the more prosperous who were moving, many neighborhoods began to deteriorate as home and apartment maintenance levels declined.

With federal help, local governments embarked on slum clearance programs and ambitious attempts to revitalize their downtown business districts. But these had disastrous effects on low-income housing. One urban planner involved in several of these urban renewal projects commented ruefully on the impact of his efforts:

(Left) A brand-new skyscraper towers over three dilapidated brownstone buildings in what has become a common example of New York City gentrification. (Below) In the East Village, squatters, surrounded by their belongings, stage a protest at the site of what used to be their home, a building that was condemned and demolished by the city government.

We were shocked to realize that the development team, including architects, had unwittingly contributed to the loss of housing once inhabited by people living on the fringes of our society. We found ourselves a part of a process of reasoned solutions for community revitalization that has been a contributing factor to the increase in homelessness.[3]

HUD estimates that by 1971 about 600,000 housing units had been swept away for parks and highways, for expensive malls, for ambitious public buildings and cultural centers.[4]

Particularly hard hit were the shabby hotels and rooming houses that offered single-room-occupancy units (SROs) that met the housing needs of many elderly home seekers and discharged mental patients. Nationwide, over a million SROs were lost between 1970 and 1982.[5] For example, in 1970 New York City had 50,000 rooms in low-cost hotels and rooming houses; by 1981 there were 19,619 such rooms. San Francisco's SRO units declined by 10,000 during the 1970s. Comparable figures can be cited in cities in all areas of the country.

The third major reason for the decline in the low-income housing stock was the wholesale abandonment of buildings by landlords during the 1960s, 1970s, and 1980s. When rents that could be obtained no longer covered the costs of running buildings, landlords walked away. Tax bills went unpaid and buildings became city property. Mortgages were foreclosed and buildings became bank property. As abandoned tenants moved out and squatters and vandals moved in, buildings became uninhabitable shells. Arson-for-profit may be a startling concept to those accustomed to thinking that only pyromaniacs and vandals set fires. But landlords did set fires—

or rather have fires started for them—to collect insurance. Hundreds of fire-gutted buildings had to be razed to the ground.

LOW-INCOME HOUSING AND THE HOUSING INDUSTRY

Why didn't the private home-building industry respond to these inroads into the low-income housing stock? After all, the owners of the tenements made fortunes from low-income rentals. But tenements can't be built any more. And the private housing industry cannot, without help from the government or other sources, build decent rental housing, offer it at rents that low-income renters can afford, and make a profit. So the industry doesn't build unsubsidized low-income rental housing.

For fifty years the nation's largest single source of low-income housing has been public housing. But authorizations for new public housing were drastically reduced in the 1980s and the new units that did become available during those years were largely the result of prior authorizations and appropriations. Should that downplaying of public housing continue? Perhaps an exploration of how well—or ill—public housing has met the needs of low-income renters will provide background for an opinion on that question.

CHAPTER THREE

THE WORLD
OF PUBLIC HOUSING

"I love the flowers," says William C. "I have them blooming all summer long." The garden borders his semi-detached duplex house, one of fifteen such units that cluster between a very posh office park and an equally posh co-op development in suburbia. Mr. C. pays an extremely low rent but he receives remarkable service. If he calls the management office, his request that a light switch be fixed will be responded to within 24 hours and the maintenance worker will check to see whether anything else needs attention.[1]

MR. C. LIVES in public housing—attractive, well-run, affordable—public housing at its best.

THE EARLY DAYS
OF PUBLIC HOUSING

The Housing Act of 1937 was landmark legislation. The plan it set up for creating public housing projects through cooperative action by federal and local governments still functions. Here's how it works.

Local public housing authorities (PHAs) have the power to acquire sites and construct multifamily public housing projects. They raise the funds for construction through the sale of tax-exempt bonds. HUD enters into contracts with the PHAs under which the federal government commits itself to make annual contributions that will pay the interest on the bonds and provide funds to retire them at their maturity dates.

HUD rules control the rent levels that may be charged in the projects and set the income limits that determine who is eligible to live in public housing.

From its launching in 1937 well into the 1960s, public housing was a successful program. Occupied primarily by families getting started on their way up in the world, they were places where "decent people could live decently." Rents brought in enough income to cover the costs of running the buildings and the projects were financially sound.

CRITICAL CHANGES

Unhappily, that situation changed. In the 1960s, as the population of the large cities in which the great majority of public housing units are located began to change, the population of the projects began to change. No longer short-term stopping places on the way to something better, they have become the housing refuge of the poorest of the working poor, the only decent available shelter for many of those on welfare.

Under present HUD rules, a two-tier eligibility system prevails. Most vacancies must go to low-income applicants, those whose incomes are below 50 percent of the area median. (*Income* always means *adjusted income,* that is, gross money income minus the deductions that are allowed for children and for elderly or handicapped persons.) Thus, in an area where the median income is $20,000, families with incomes up to $10,000 are eligible. A small percentage of units may be rented to so-called lower income households, that is, families with incomes between 50 and 80 percent of the median for the area. Thus, a few families with incomes as high as $16,000 could be admitted.

Actually, in large cities, between one-half and two-thirds of the tenants are on welfare and the tenant rolls at the Bankhead Courts project in Atlanta are not untypical.[2] Here children and young people under 19 make up the majority of the residents—1,025 out of 1,700. Ninety-eight percent of the households are headed by women. Of the 675 adults, 42 have jobs. These are people who, far from looking ahead to moves to better housing, are predominantly settled in for life.

As the percentage of project tenants living on some form of public assistance rose, even the low rents of the projects became, for many, too heavy a burden. To ease that problem, Congress passed, in 1969, the so-called "Brooke Amendment," which limited public housing rents to 25 percent of tenant households' incomes. This percentage was raised in 1982 to 30 percent. Rents at these levels cover only about half the costs of operating the projects, so from 1969 onward the federal government has paid annual operating subsidies to public housing authorities.

HOW GOOD/HOW BAD ARE THE PROJECTS?

Robert Taylor Houses in Chicago is the nation's largest housing project—twenty-eight sixteen-story buildings on ninety-two acres. One-half of one percent of Chicago's population live in Robert Taylor, but in a recent year it was the scene for 11 percent of the city's murders and 9 percent of its rapes.[3] The Robert Taylor figures are frequently cited and the horror stories that emanate from the projects from time to time get wide press coverage. Thus, when a nine-year-old asthmatic Chicago child died in a project because paramedics, pelted with eggs, refused to enter a project building until police arrived to cover them, the story made the headlines. When a housing project in Atlanta lost its mail delivery service because a mail carrier got caught in a drug battle, that story, too, made the headlines.

It is understandable that there is a widely held perception of public housing projects as high-rise apartment

This photo was taken in 1970, shortly after two policemen were ambushed and killed in Seward Park in front of the Cabrini-Green public housing project in Chicago. At the time, the complex's 3,500 apartments housed 18,000 persons.

buildings where garbage gets thrown out of windows, welfare checks are likely to be stolen from mailboxes, people step around pools of urine in the hallways, and unsupervised youngsters hassle frightened oldsters. Indeed, some projects are so ineffectively managed, so run down, so badly maintained, so plagued by crime and vandalism that, despite the low-income housing squeeze there are, nationwide, thousands of vacancies in public housing.

But there is the other side of the coin. Many public housing projects, like William C.'s, are low-rise structures indistinguishable from the buildings around them; high-rise projects are no longer being built. A comprehensive program of modernization is under way although it has been hampered by unsteady and diminishing funding. Knowledgeable people estimate that no more than 5 percent of project tenants are serious threats to their neighbors. In sum, the 1.4 million housing units in over 10,000 housing projects provide decent, affordable housing for the great majority of their residents, who are preponderantly large families, the elderly, the poorest of the poor.

PROBLEM PEOPLE

A digression about people is essential here. If 5 percent of the tenants in public housing are threats to their neighbors because of their criminal activities, there are others who make life in the projects less pleasant than it would be if they were not around. There are problem families—not just in housing projects, of course—families whose housekeeping standards, child-rearing practices, and personal behavior are such that peaceful coexistence with their neighbors is almost impossible. One housing expert has observed that the most serious manpower need in public housing is for professionals who can remotivate and retrain problem families for successful community life.

One other point about improving people: better housing does not work miracles. The problem family moved from substandard housing to vastly improved housing does not, experts tell us, become a different family unless significant guidance and support services also enter the picture. When improved living conditions remove obstacles that were keeping family members from living as they know how to live, from doing the good things they wanted to do, housing makes a difference and better housing does work magic.

NEW PRESSURES ON PUBLIC HOUSING

The doubling up of families referred to in chapter 1 has placed an especially heavy burden on public housing because that's where so many of the evicted do the doubling up. Clean-up costs rise dramatically when project populations soar; household appliances getting doubly heavy use have to be replaced more frequently; operating costs generally escalate. Housing officials in one major city admitted their awareness of some 100,000 illegal occupants in their buildings but argued this way: We know what's going on, and it's hurting us. We're running an operating deficit but we're not even going to ask HUD for more money. They'll just say where's your plan to get the illegal tenants out of your buildings? We haven't got any such plans. Where will they go? Out on the street, of course. There isn't any other place.

These days drug use, drug dealing, and the violence they generate have moved to the top of the list of public housing worries. Project managers complain of

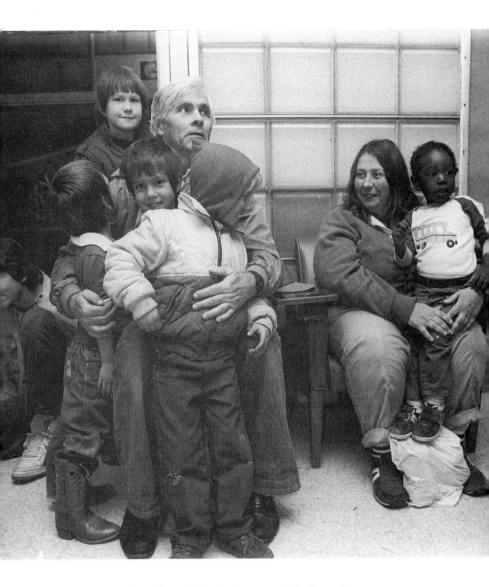

Melvin and Gloria Perry, who both work
but can't afford a place to live, play with
homeless children at the Salvation Army
Family Emergency Shelter in Reno, Nevada.

inadequate police presence and lack of funds to buy security. They complain especially that efforts to remove drug dealers from apartment bases within the projects are often hampered by required eviction procedures. Those procedures, originally created to protect tenants from unwarranted removal from their homes, can cause a drug eviction case to drag on for two or three years. Furthermore, when the eviction procedure includes a hearing, witnesses who know what has been going on in a drug dealer's base are often afraid to testify because the threat of retaliation is so frightening.

Housing officials are doubtless watching with interest how New York City will fare with its recent drug busting initiative: the use of federal racketeering laws to fight drug traffic in its housing projects. One of the situations that frustrated law-abiding residents most was that drug sweeps and arrests were frequently followed by the prompt return of the arrested dealers to their apartment bases and the reopening of business. Under federal racketeering laws, property used in illegal activities can be seized and forfeited. By obtaining warrants under these laws, apartments used for drug traffic can be seized and leases forfeited.

It's interesting to note that one of Jack Kemp's early moves after his appointment as secretary of HUD was to send a memorandum to the heads of the 3,000 public housing authorities asking for a report on "what you are doing to evict drug abusers and drug dealers from your projects."

PUBLIC HOUSING—AN ENDANGERED SPECIES OF LOW-INCOME HOUSING?

The reduced levels at which operating costs are being subsidized by the federal government have brought public housing to a critical state. The needed repairs and modernization revealed by HUD's 1987 study carry a price tag of some $20 billion. Because that kind of expenditure is not being embarked upon, thousands of public housing units are being demolished as beyond repair. And as the graph below shows, since federal support for new subsidized public housing has been declining steadily over the past ten years, public housing's contribution to the supply of low-income housing has gone down and is likely to continue to do so.

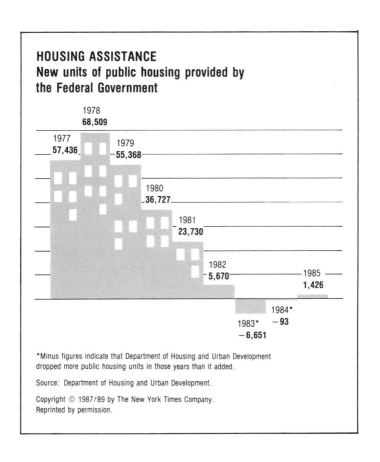

HOUSING ASSISTANCE
New units of public housing provided by the Federal Government

1978
68,509

1977
57,436

1979
55,368

1980
36,727

1981
23,730

1982
5,670

1985
1,426

1984*
−93

1983*
−6,651

*Minus figures indicate that Department of Housing and Urban Development dropped more public housing units in those years than it added.

Source: Department of Housing and Urban Development.

Copyright © 1987/89 by The New York Times Company. Reprinted by permission.

Another hazard lies ahead for public housing. HUD's contracts with PHAs covering funding for construction are forty-year commitments. When they have run their course, the bonds whose sale produced the funds for construction will have matured and been paid off. The projects, by the terms of the contracts, then belong to the PHAs, who are theoretically free to convert them to other types of housing. To the extent that they do, the supply of low-income housing will be still further reduced.

Most commentators on the nation's housing situation, even those who consider new public housing an unacceptably expensive solution to the low-income housing crisis, agree that the *existing* stock must be rehabilitated and preserved, that badly managed projects must be turned around, that terrorism in the projects must be eradicated. And the new winds that are stirring in some of the nation's projects revive memories of public housing as a way up rather than a dead end.

For example, the possibilities that tenant management opens up are suggested by the Cochran Gardens experience in St. Louis. There, a tenant management group transformed a project so bad the city wanted to tear it down into a showcase of cleanliness and security. The group went on to create a catering business, five day-care centers, and a cable television installation service, all of which employ residents from within the project. The tenant team is now at work on negotiations to transform Cochran Gardens from a public housing project to cooperative apartments owned by the present tenants.

Consider the possibilities if the idealism of Robert Armstrong, Omaha's new housing authority head, were to spread. Acting on his conviction that education is the key to better lives, he pushes the young people in his projects to achieve success in school, and pushes their parents to get behind them. Study centers within the projects offer tutoring. A project pupil's perfect attendance wins a savings bond; high achievement can earn a scholarship. If the children in a family are truants, the family faces eviction. "We must make sure," says Armstrong, "that the children of public housing don't become housing adults."

Public housing remains a key component of the nation's housing stock. But expenditures for public housing are no longer the major component of the government's housing outlays. Far more federal money now goes into programs that help low-income renters move into *privately* owned housing that they could not afford on their own.

CHAPTER FOUR

THE VOUCHER IDEA

When Pearl R. heard that her landlord was going to do a lot of face-lifting in her Chicago apartment building, she wondered why. As far as Pearl was concerned, no improvement was needed. Her bright, clean, one-bedroom apartment was her pride and joy. She had not been able to believe her luck when the building opened, twenty years before, and she had been one of the applicants, out of the hundreds on the waiting list, who had been accepted as a tenant.

The neighbors were whispering that "he paid off the mortgage," but Pearl couldn't see how that could have anything to do with her. Two months later she received notice that her rent was being raised from $300 to $750.

Neighbors whose rent increases had put them in the same boat assured Pearl that "we've asked everybody. There's not a thing we can do. He's got the right to raise our rent this way."

As her landlord had expected, Pearl moved out.

Hᴏᴡ ᴄᴏᴜʟᴅ Pearl R.'s story have happened? The answer lies in the government's efforts to involve the private housing industry in providing low-income housing.

ENGAGING THE PRIVATE SECTOR

In the 1960s public housing began to lose its appeal as a response to the nation's low-income housing needs. Housing advocates in Congress, instead of asking for additional billions to construct more public housing, began to argue this way: So far, the only major effort made to provide low-income housing has been public housing. Why not turn to the private housing industry? We know that private builders, on their own, can't produce housing units and offer them at rents low-income households can afford. But if the federal government were to subsidize the private builders, they could.

The argument was persuasive. During the 1960s and early 1970s housing bills were passed offering a variety of inducements to developers: loans at below market-rate interest, mortgage insurance, tax breaks that made investment in housing attractive. In return, builders agreed to maintain rent levels affordable to low-income tenants.

Over 600,000 housing units were produced under contracts based on this legislation, but the programs were extremely costly and many projects ended in mortgage foreclosure. The most serious flaw, however, was a clause written into many of the contracts—a clause that is turning out to be a time bomb.

Builders were given the right to pay off subsidized mortgages at the end of twenty years. Such a pay-off ends a builder's obligation to the government; he is free to raise rents, convert the building to a co-op, do with it what he pleases. As Pearl R.'s case illustrates, the twenty-year anniversary has already arrived for a number of projects, the mortgages have been paid off, and the housing units turned to more profitable use.

Not all of the 600,000 low-income units are subject to prepayment and not all owners will want to prepay. But those in areas where the private housing market would make possible higher rents than they are now being allowed to charge are very likely to want to do so. HUD estimates that prepayment could remove 363,000 units from the low-income housing stock; of that number it estimates that 154,300 units very likely will be so lost.[1]

Congress responded to this threat by enacting legislation in 1987 that, in effect, placed a two-year moratorium on pay-offs. The housing industry, as might be expected, argued that builders had complied with their part of the bargain with the federal government and that changing the prepayment rules was unfair.

Meanwhile, states in which large numbers of low-income renters would be affected by mortgage prepayments have evolved a number of solutions to the problem. Five states have bought up mortgages, presumably so that they, as the creditors, can refuse prepayment. Another state offers a tax break if, after paying off the mortgage, the developer sells the building to a nonprofit organization that promises to maintain below-market rents and to restrict tenancy to low-income families. Another state is helping tenants in a threatened building to buy it and run it themselves.

OTHER PRIVATE
SECTOR INITIATIVES

Legislation passed in 1974 took a different tack to persuade developers to build new low-income projects—the *Section 8 New Housing Program,* or to rehabilitate deteriorated buildings and rent them to low-income tenants—the *Section 8 Substantial Rehabilitation Program.*

Developers participating in those two programs entered into fifteen- to forty-year contracts with the federal government under which they agreed to rent their new or rehabilitated apartments to tenants who met the HUD income limits. Each apartment was covered by a Section 8 Certificate given to the builder. The certificate guaranteed that the developer would receive a rent subsidy for that apartment—a subsidy high enough so that the tenant's rent payment (30 percent of family income) plus the government subsidy would equal a *fair market rent.* The fair market rents were set at a level high enough to ensure that a developer's rental income would cover all the costs related to a building, that is, pay-off of construction or rehabilitation costs as well as current operating costs.

Obviously these programs were unduly costly. There was no incentive built into the programs for builders to keep costs low. Whatever their costs, the fair market rents would ensure their recovery. Flaws like this in housing legislation should be kept in mind while reading the unhappy saga of HUD's recent years. Many programs have far too many opportunities for fraud and inefficiency built right into them, weaknesses that must be rigorously excised. Fortunately, that process seems to be under way.

The Section 8 New Housing and Section 8 Substantial Rehabilitation programs were terminated in 1983. But the 791,000 units of low-income housing they created are in use—and in jeopardy. The expiration dates for the contracts under which they were built fall between 1985 and 2025. In areas where building owners know they can get higher rents, they may not choose to renew the contracts. If they do not, their rent-regulated apartments will be lost to the low-income rental housing stock.

SECTION 8 EXISTING HOUSING PROGRAM

The Section 8 New Housing program just described was an attempt to get more low-income housing units *built* by the private sector. Section 8 Existing Housing is a program that puts low-income renters into *existing* housing units they could not afford on their own and pays part of the rent for them. This Section 8 program is very much alive and by 1981 was providing affordable housing for about 973,000 households.[2]

The income requirements to receive Section 8 housing assistance are the same as for admission to public housing. In other words, the adjusted income of a family applying for Section 8 assistance cannot exceed 50 percent of the median income of the area in which the family lives.

A household that applies for Section 8 assistance, and qualifies, receives a Certificate of Family Participation, which states that the household will be given a rent subsidy. Certificate in hand, the family must find a housing unit that it wishes to rent—but not just any housing unit. It must meet two requirements: (1) The condition of the unit must meet the quality standards that the local housing authority has established. (2) The rent asked for the unit must not exceed the figure set by HUD as the fair market rent for units of its size in that area. A family usually has sixty days in which to find an acceptable unit; if it fails to do so, it loses its certificate. When an acceptable unit is found and the landlord agrees to accept the Section 8 tenant, a contract with the landlord specifies that the tenant will pay 30 percent of the family income as rent and the balance will come from the local public housing authority.

Actually, in about half the Section 8 rentals, the sequence of events suggested above—obtain a certificate and then find an apartment—is not the way things happen. About half the subsidy recipients are so-called "in-place" tenants. The Doe family, for example, whose income was $600 a month, hung on to their apartment even when the rent went up to $425 a month. They preferred rigid economies on food and other necessities to a futile hunt for comparable quarters elsewhere. When they finally obtained a Section 8 certificate and their landlord agreed to their staying on a Section 8 basis, their monthly outlay for rent dropped to $180, the required 30 percent of their income; the remaining $245 of their rent was paid by the local PHA.

The housing units involved in Section 8 rentals are very different from public housing's mammoth projects. More than half are single-family houses. The second largest category of Section 8 housing consists of apartments in buildings of two to six rental units. Typically these houses and apartments are owned by landlords operating on a very small scale. More than a third of them own just one rental unit; fewer than half own more than ten units.

HOUSING VOUCHERS

The Reagan administration introduced and strongly supported the newest form of low-income rental housing assistance: vouchers. These are very similar to Section 8 certificates, in that they can be used to cover a portion of the rent on any units voucher holders find that meet local PHA standards. Vouchers differ from Section 8 certificates, however, in one important way: they give assisted renters more flexibility in the use of their housing assistance. For example, assume that three families with housing vouchers have adjusted family incomes of $1,000 each. Family A finds an apartment it likes for which the landlord is asking $400. HUD guidelines set the *payment standard* for apartments of the size and in the location they have chosen at $400. (The payment standard in the voucher program is always the same as the fair market rent, the rent that HUD has set for apartments of that size in that area.) Family A's housing voucher entitles it to receive a housing subsidy equal to the difference between 30 percent of its income, $300, and the payment standard for its apartment, $400. That is, its subsidy is $100; its out-of-pocket expenditure for housing will be $300.

Family B is lucky enough to find an apartment that rents for $350 although the payment standard for the apartment is $400. Family B's housing voucher entitles it to the difference between 30 percent of its income and the payment standard for its apartment. So its housing subsidy, just like Family A's, will be $100, but its out-of-pocket rent expense will be only $250.

Family C is not satisfied with any apartment it can find for $400 or less and finally decides on a unit for which the landlord insists on getting $500, even though it is in the $400 standard payment category. Since its housing subsidy is the same as the other two families, its out-of-pocket rent expense will be $400.

The mechanics of getting certificates and vouchers into the hands of families are delegated by HUD to local public housing authorities. The PHAs invite applications and work with public and private welfare agencies to spread the word about the programs so that qualified, needy households will apply. The opportunities for misuse of such programs are obvious. Unless the officials who administer them are determined that only the most worthy applicants be served, others, less worthy, will receive housing assistance.

It is the local PHAs that enter into contracts with the landlords in whose buildings certificates and vouchers are used. Section 8 certificate contracts run for fifteen years, voucher contracts for five years. The PHAs send out the subsidy checks to landlords, the money they dispense coming from HUD. Complicated? Yes, indeed, but as landlords have been known to observe: "The tenants may be late with their share of the rent but the subsidy checks get here on time."

SECTION 8 AND VOUCHERS
VS. OTHER FORMS
OF HOUSING ASSISTANCE

A major argument advanced for certificate and voucher plans is that they will encourage rehabilitation of rental housing. The point has been made that landlords abandon buildings because the rents they can get do not cover their operating and maintenance costs. Abandoned buildings deteriorate and are soon out of the rental housing stock. If, so the argument goes, landlords are assured that certificates and vouchers will produce rental income high enough to maintain their buildings, they will think twice before abandoning them; they will reclaim and rehabilitate them. Actually, during its brief period of operation, the Section 8 Substantial Rehabilitation program motivated only a very modest percentage of reclamations. A Moderate Rehabilitation component in the Section 8 program offers rent subsidies and tax credits to owners who undertake less substantial rehabilitation of buildings to make them eligible for participation in the rent subsidy program. This is the program from which headline stories emerged of $400,000 "consulting fees" paid to influence peddlers for telephone calls to their powerful friends within HUD. The projects selected for subsidy were supposed to be chosen competitively, but it now appears that builders with well-connected consultants could obtain project approvals without undergoing the rigors of competition.

When the Moderate Rehabilitation influence-peddling stories broke, Housing Secretary Jack Kemp suspended funds for the program and canceled most of the contracts that had been negotiated for the current fiscal year. When the program was reactivated, a system for numerical scoring of rehabilitation proposals was in place to assure genuinely competitive award of contracts.

Advocates of the certificate/voucher approach to low-income housing assistance also maintain that a given sum of money spent on these consumer-oriented programs will serve twice as many households as the same sum of money used for construction of new housing units.

On the other hand, certificate/voucher programs work only if vacant apartments are available that meet the quality and rent standards set by legislation and HUD administrators. In Boston and New York, for example, two cities with extremely tight rental markets, 62 percent of the households holding housing vouchers in early 1987 could not find housing in which to use them. Nationwide, it is estimated that 25 percent of the vouchers and certificates issued go unused.[3]

Renters who are enjoying Section 8 certificates and vouchers face the same running-out-of-contracts threat that confronts tenants enjoying lower-than-market rents in buildings constructed under federal subsidy contracts. However, housing experts who worry about landlords opting out of contracts so they can put their buildings to more profitable use have little fear that Congress will fail to authorize renegotiation of consumer-held housing assistance contracts.

THE HOUSING ASSISTANCE LOTTERY

Amy, a single mother, lives in an apartment in Bigtown with her two children. Beatrice, another single mother, lives in an apartment in Metropolis with her two children. The rent for both apartments is the same—$300. The welfare checks that are the sole support for both families include a housing allowance of $250. Amy pays her landlord $250 from her welfare check; he receives the remaining $50 from the local PHA. Beatrice pays all her $300 rent from her welfare check, which means that she has $50 less for other necessities than Amy has. Why does Amy get housing assistance when Beatrice does not? The answer is, pure chance. Metropolis may have so many Section 8 applicants that Beatrice's name is way down on the waiting list for a certificate. Or maybe she had a certificate and wasn't able to find an apartment she liked that would take a Section 8 tenant. Pure chance.

Housing assistance of any kind has always been a matter of chance in the United States. To put that another way, there has never been a housing assistance *entitlement program* in this country. The essential characteristic of an entitlement program is this: The law establishing the program says that anyone who meets *these requirements* is to receive *this assistance*. The food stamp program is an entitlement program. Anyone who meets the income requirements for food stamps and applies for them, gets them. When the budget is made, an appropriation for food stamps must be included that will cover the number of qualified people who are expected to ask for them. The only way for the government to get out of that obligation is to change the law.

Nobody ever proposed a public housing bill that said: "Projects are to be constructed in a quantity large enough so that all households who qualify and apply for public housing can be accepted." The million households now on waiting lists for public housing know this all too well. Rather, housing assistance bills take a different tack: "Local public housing authorities will be helped to build public housing projects. PHAs are invited to apply to HUD." When the budget is being made, Congress decides how much money to allow for new public housing. HUD looks at that number, looks at the applications it has received, tells three PHAs that they can go ahead and tells all the others, "We regret to inform you that. . . ."

Section 8 certificates are not available to every household whose income is below 50 percent of the median in the area. HUD regulations simply say that no household may be given a certificate unless its income

In Chicago, an estimated crowd of 5,000
people gather in the street, waiting to
apply for federally subsidized housing.

is below that level. In making the budget, Congress is bound to honor Section 8 certificates that were issued in previous years and appropriate enough funds to cover them, but the number of new certificates issued in any year is entirely up to Congress and the president. In 1988, for example, HUD had 18,000 new certificates to distribute among all the 50 states.

Housing assistance is indeed a lottery. In 1983 (the latest year for which these data are currently available) 12.9 million renter households met the "below 50 percent of the area median" income level eligibility standard. Only 28 percent of those families were receiving assistance under federal housing programs.[4] A simpler and reasonably accurate way to say that: One out of four renter households who needs housing assistance gets it.

How are the rest of the renter households faring— the three out of four eligible families who don't get housing assistance, the almost-eligible families who get no assistance, and the moderate-income renter families? How are they all faring? Not very well, as we shall see.

CHAPTER FIVE

RENTERS ON THEIR OWN

In the 1980s housing has become the great divider of haves from have-nots. A have is somebody who owns his own home, and effortlessly increases his net worth as the value of the house inflates. A have-not is a tenant of moderate means, vulnerable to a shrinking supply of rental housing, the threat of condo conversion, and steadily escalating rent costs.[1]

A SQUEEZE on renters in general, not just low-income renters, began in the 1970s. Between 1970 and 1983 the median income of renters rose 100 percent, but in that same period the median rent rose 192 percent. This disparity continued, and by 1988 five million households were paying over 35 percent of their income for rent; another six million households were paying more than half their incomes.[2]

WHY THE RENTAL SQUEEZE?

Continuing upward pressure on rents is an inevitable consequence of the spread between the demand for and the supply of rental housing in many parts of the country. Two major factors are at work on the demand side. In the 1970s and 1980s many of the baby-boom generation moved into the twenty-one to thirty-five age group, a group that traditionally produces many new households seeking rental units. Second, for reasons that will be explored in the next chapter, many in that age group, who would in other times have been home buyers, remain renters.

Supply simply has not kept up with demand in the rental market. Instead of going up, production of rental housing has gone down. Between 1970 and 1977, 57 percent of the new housing started in the United States was rental housing; in the 1980s it dropped to 9 percent.[3] Then there is the co-op boom. Just as abandonment of buildings reduces the low-income rental housing stock, conversion of rental buildings to cooperatives and condominiums drastically cuts down the supply of higher scale rental units. Even before a co-op or condo conversion takes place, "warehousing" of rental units starts to reduce the rental stock. That is, when tenants move out, owners hold the apartments vacant instead of renting them because vacant apartments can be sold for significantly higher prices than the insider prices landlords are required to offer residents.

SUBSTANDARD HOUSING CONDITIONS

A rent squeeze is not the only housing problem that currently vexes renters. Maintenance of the public spaces and apartments in their buildings may have deteriorated.

While it is true that over 40 percent of the substandard housing units in the nation are in rural areas and that a substantial number of those units are owner-occupied, renters are the occupants of more than half the 7.6 million housing units that are classified by HUD as substandard.[4]

Some background is essential here, however, to compare where the nation *is* in terms of the physical condition of its housing stock with where it *was* as recently as 1940. And one needs to go back only about a hundred years before that to find housing conditions that are almost unbelievable. An 1857 report on conditions in urban tenements included phrases like these: "dim, undrained courts oozing with pollution," "dark narrow stairways, decayed with age, reeking with filth, overrun with vermin," "rotted floors, ceilings often too low to permit you to stand upright," "windows stuffed with rags."

Building codes, health and sanitation standards, and fire regulations have made such deplorable housing a thing of the past, but as late as 1940, 45 percent of the housing units in the United States lacked complete bathrooms and kitchens, 18 percent were "dilapidated," that is, "in visibly unsatisfactory physical condition."[5] By 1987 units without kitchens and bathrooms had dropped to only 2.4 percent of the housing stock and the dilapidated percentage had gone down also.[6]

There is disturbing evidence, however, that the condition of the nation's housing stock has been allowed to slip in the recent years of housing pressure. HUD's housing survey (until recently made annually) collects data on "housing maintenance and upkeep," using nine "indicators" of unsatisfactory levels of maintenance. The indicators are: some or all wiring exposed, lacking working outlets in some rooms, cracks or holes in walls or ceilings, holes in interior floors, roof leaks, signs of rats or mice, recent breakdowns in water supply, recent breakdown in sewer/septic cesspool systems, and recent periods of inadequate heat. Between 1974 and 1981 HUD found that the number of dwelling units in which working outlets were lacking in some rooms went down; the number found to have exposed wiring remained at the same level; but the number of units with cracks or holes in walls, floors, or ceilings, the number of leaky roofs— all up. The incidence of breakdowns in water supply, of breakdowns in sewer or cesspool systems, the episodes of inadequate heat—all up. Furthermore, while the num-

Cholera, diphtheria, and starvation were
the constant companions of immigrant families
who lived in New York City's crowded, squalid
tenement dwellings around the turn of the century.

ber of housing units without complete kitchens and/or bathrooms showed the downward trend reported above, the number of units with no heating equipment went up.

RESPONSE TO TENANT PROBLEMS

As the ranks of renters with problems have been joined by increasing numbers of politically informed and involved middle-class families, tenant organization and tenant activism have likewise increased—with some results. A number of state laws now assure tenants that:

- if you do not receive essential services like heat, you do not have to pay your rent
- you can not be evicted simply because you complain about conditions in your building
- the landlord can not shut off your utilities, or lock you out of your apartment, or seize your possessions

By 1981, twenty-four states had enacted legislation protecting the rights of tenants in buildings where the landlord has started moving toward conversion to a co-op or condo. While the laws vary, their general thrust is to protect tenants, particularly the elderly, who can't afford to buy their apartments and to ensure the reasonableness of the terms on which apartments are offered for sale.

The cause most vigorously pursued by tenant associations, however, is rent control. Protecting rent control legislation from dilution and monitoring the boards charged with setting allowable rent increases are concerns understandably close to the hearts and pockets of renters.

THE CASE AGAINST RENT CONTROL

Many large cities in the United States have rent control, that is, some system under which a government agency, at predetermined intervals, sets the percentages at which rents will be allowed to rise. The effects of rent control on the rental market is a highly controversial issue.

Those who oppose it refer to rent control in terms such as "a legal jamming device placed to intercept the message sent by consumers of housing to the providers of housing." Thus, high on the list of arguments against rent control is the assertion that it discourages the construction of rental housing. Rising rents, the argument goes, send a message from consumers of housing to the providers of housing that more rental units are needed; that if units are produced they will be taken, at rents that will bring a profit-making return to the developer. But, the argument continues, where there are controls on rents, builders are convinced that the regulatory boards will not adjust rents upward to keep pace with rising operating costs. So they don't build rental housing.

The same line of argument seems to support the assertion that rent control encourages the conversion of apartment buildings to cooperatives or condominiums. Landlords squeezed between rising costs of operating their buildings and rents held down by controls are likely to opt for the quick profit that can be garnered from conversions.

The arguments against rent control are not couched solely in terms of the reaction of landlords. The interests of renters themselves are invoked. Rent control, say its

A tenant enjoys her newly converted co-op apartment in Park Slope, Brooklyn, while below, several families pose in front of their new building in Manhattan's Lower East Side. The families were chosen to buy into the first cooperative apartments built exclusively for the homeless.

opponents, so distorts the rental market that it freezes tenants in their present apartments. As one analyst put it: "It's a kind of musical-chairs game where the music has stopped." Controlled rents are held so far below market rates for new rental housing that there is no incentive for tenants to move to new buildings.

For example, suppose a family is living in a two-bedroom, two-bath apartment in a pleasant area for which the regulated rent is $675. Unregulated, the apartment would probably rent for, say, $955. A new apartment building is constructed nearby on a site that commands a beautiful view of a lake. The kitchens, baths, and lobby in the new building are far more attractive than those in the older building; the services it offers—twenty-four-hour doorman service, for example—are far superior. A two-bedroom, two-bath apartment with a balcony overlooking the lake is offered at $1,250. The family in the $675 apartment can well afford the $1,250 rent, but the idea of giving up their bargain rental is unthinkable. Had they been paying $955, they might make the move.

Landlords' associations repeatedly cite inequities like this: couples whose children are grown and gone continue to live in large rent-regulated apartments because they can't find a small apartment, which they would prefer, at the rent they pay for their large apartment. Meanwhile, a growing family faces increasing discomfort because they can't find a larger apartment at a reasonably higher rent than their present regulated rent.

Rent regulation, its opponents maintain, protects the wrong people. They cite a recent survey conducted for landlords in New York City, which has the most comprehensive rent regulation program in the nation. Looking at the poorest and the richest fourths of the city's renters, the study found that two-thirds of the poorest households pay more than 40 percent of their incomes for rent. Only one percent of the richest households had that heavy a rental burden; 92 percent of the richest group paid one-quarter or less of their incomes for rent.[7]

As further evidence of the flaws inherent in rent regulation, opponents cite the fact that in New York City rent-stabilized apartments are so prized that landlords can extort so-called "key money" from a tenant moving into a newly vacated apartment; with a dozen people competing for the vacancy it's easy for the landlord to get a quite substantial sum under the table.

THE CASE FOR RENT CONTROL

The case advanced by advocates of rent control is very simple: it is needed. Renters need protection against the escalation that would occur were rentals opened up to market forces. Nobody questions the need to regulate the rates of telephone and lighting companies, because if there is only one seller of a service, consumers must be protected against that seller gouging them. In tight rental markets, with extremely low vacancy rates, renters don't have the opportunity to compare and choose that must exist if a market is to be deemed free. So they must be protected against those who would gouge the helpless.

Furthermore, proponents argue, a change in public policy from rent regulation to a free rental market would cause such a massive upheaval that unacceptable hardship for unacceptable numbers of people would be inevitable.

"Rent control is needed" is indeed a simple argument. But it is politically powerful. There are more tenant voters than landlord voters.

Gradual modification of rent control, however, is not unthinkable. Again, to cite New York City, the vacancy rate for apartments renting at over $750 a month rose to over 5 percent in 1988 and landlords were quick to press for decontrol at that level.[8] They were unsuccessful, but the effort will surely be pressed again, particularly if vacancy rates at the upper end of the rental scale continue to rise.

Nationwide, however, abandonment of rent control in cities where it is current policy is unlikely.

CHAPTER SIX

THE PLIGHT
OF THE WOULD-BE
HOME BUYER

"I had to give up my dream of a center-hall colonial to afford a house in a good school district. . . . We got an ugly house with a leaky basement—but what did I expect for a quarter-million dollars?"[1]   Roxanne L.

ROXANNE L. sounds bitter, but her family did buy a house. In recent years, thousands of other would-be buyers simply gave up. In 1980, 65 percent of American households were living in homes that they owned. From 1980 onward, at least 800,000 households that wanted to buy homes gave up the attempt. Home ownership no longer stands at 65 percent.[2]

HOW A HIGH LEVEL OF HOME OWNERSHIP WAS ACHIEVED

In 1940, 44 percent of American families were home owners, but the housing boom that began after World War II soon changed that picture. The boom was triggered by the enormous backlog of demand for housing that had built up during the war years, but it was possible only because a new way of financing the purchase of homes had been created as part of the New Deal.

The housing industry had just about gone under during the Great Depression. One reason for its collapse was the then-existing mortgage system. Nothing longer than a five-year mortgage was available, and large down payments were routinely required. During the term of the mortgage the borrower usually paid only interest; at the end of five years he had to pay off the face amount of the loan—the so-called balloon payment—or renegotiate the mortgage. In the early 1930s half of all outstanding home mortgages were in default and foreclosures were running at almost 1,000 per working day.

The National Housing Act of 1934 changed all that. A new government agency, the Federal Housing Administration (FHA), was created. Its basic purpose was to insure mortgage loans and thus attract capital into the housing industry. Traditionally, if a home buyer could not meet the obligations of a mortgage loan, the lender's only recourse was to foreclose and try to recover what was owed by selling the property. When the real estate market was weak, lenders often didn't fare very well. Mortgage insurance eliminated that risk. A foreclosed FHA-insured mortgage loan is paid off out of FHA insurance funds.

A totally new kind of mortgage was created, a mortgage that would run for as long as twenty years and would be amortized—interest and principal paid off—by monthly payments over the term of the mortgage.

The original twenty-year mortgage term and the original 20 percent down payment requirement for FHA mortgages were substantially liberalized over the years, but from the beginning the system did what it was supposed to do. It attracted into the housing industry the huge amounts of capital that supported a housing boom well into the 1960s.

THE FHA TODAY

Today the buyer of a single-family house can obtain a thirty-year FHA-insured mortgage up to a limit of $67,500. (In high-cost areas the ceilings are higher.) Required down payments are low—3 percent on a house costing under $50,000; above that price, the buyer must come up with 3 percent of the first $25,000 and 5 percent of the remainder. Interest rates for FHA mortgages are no longer regulated but left to be determined by market forces.

The importance of the FHA-insured mortgage in the housing market has fallen off considerably. Many so-called conventional mortgages (mortgages not backed by any government agency) are now competitive with FHA mortgages in down-payment ratios and interest rates and are free from the red tape that accompanies government-involved programs. Furthermore, higher home prices have put a substantial part of the housing market outside FHA mortgage ceilings. But legislation is currently moving through Congress to raise those ceilings.

THE DOWNWARD TREND IN HOME OWNERSHIP

Home ownership continued to rise in the 1970s, but a significant shift in that trend took place in the 1980s:

	Percentage of U.S. Home Ownership
1981	65.4
1982	64.8
1983	64.6
1984	64.5
1985	64.1
1986	63.8

Source: David C. Schwartz, Richard C. Ferlauto, and Daniel N. Hoffman, *A New Housing Policy for America: Recapturing the American Dream.* (Philadelphia: Temple University Press, 1988), p. 7.

Those figures signal no change in American attitudes concerning home ownership. Surveys of housing preferences continue to show that an almost universal part of the American dream is to own a home.

Any decline in home ownership is significant, so the importance of that overall drop of 1.6 percent should not be minimized. But the figures below are more significant. Consider the age groups whose declining ability to buy a home contributed most heavily to the overall figure.

Age of Householder	Percentage of Home Ownership		
	1981	1986	% Change
Under 25	20.7	17.2	−3.5
25–29*	41.7	36.7	−5.0
30–34*	59.3	53.6	−5.7
35–39*	68.9	64.8	−4.1
40–44	73.7	70.5	−3.2
45–49	76.2	74.1	−2.1

*Members of the baby-boom generation

Source: David C. Schwartz, et al, p. 7.

Clearly, members of the baby-boom generation have been having more trouble becoming home owners than their parents had. Understandably so, because in terms of income trends, the baby boomers' parents had rosier prospects and did much better than they are doing. Income history indicates that in 1950 a typical thirty-year old could expect that ten years later he would be earning 58 percent more than his present wage; he could expect another 44 percent increase by the time he was fifty. The average forty-year-old in 1987 was only 21 percent better off than he had been in 1977. Wages are no longer on the escalator of an earlier day. This too is understandable because the rise in productivity of American workers has slowed.

WHAT IT TAKES NOWADAYS TO BUY A HOUSE

The most important reason for the inability of many young people to buy their first homes in the late 1970s and 1980s is the fact that in many parts of the country home prices rose so much more rapidly than incomes that houses simply became unaffordable.

The 1987 figures from the National Association of Home Builders given below suggest why so many families can't afford to buy. The figures are based on these assumptions, which are typical of current practice: (1) the lending bank will require a 10 percent down payment; (2) the buyer will need a thirty-year mortgage, which will be offered at 11 percent; (3) the bank will insist that the buyer's income be high enough so that mortgage payments do not exceed 28 percent of income.

To buy a house priced at	the buyer needs, for down payment and closing costs	the buyer must have an income of (qualifying income)
$100,000	$16,000	$43,187
250,000	40,000	102,621
400,000	64,000	164,177

Source: Carol Vogel, "The High Cost of Housing,"
The New York Times Magazine, June 26, 1987.

In 1987 there were 15,008,000 families in which the head of the family was between twenty-five and thirty-four, traditionally prime home buying years. Only 3,080,000 of those families had incomes of $45,000 or above that would put them in a position to buy a $100,000 house. And $100,000 homes are rare birds in many parts of the country. For example, consider a more specific, localized situation. In Massachusetts, 75 percent of the state's population could afford to buy a home at the 1977 median price. In 1987 the median price of homes being offered for sale was $170,000 and only 6 percent of the population could afford to buy.[3]

It must be emphasized that regional differences in the real estate market are sharp. When figures for the whole country are used, housing sounds affordable. The National Association of Realtors computes an *affordability index* so comparisons of housing affordability can be made over a period of years. When the index number stands at 100, this is what it means: the median income of households in the United States is 100 percent of the qualifying income needed to purchase a home at the median home price then prevailing in the market. In September 1988 the index was at 113.3, which meant that median income was well above median home price. Housing was, theoretically, affordable.

That statistic is meaningless, of course, for thousands of would-be first-time home buyers. For example, take the situation of two cities—Houston and New York—cited in the chart on page 79. The median family income in Houston is $37,059 compared to $33,203 in New York; but, whereas the median price for a home in Houston is $65,800, the median home price in New York is an astronomical $178,500. The New York resident will have to be earning a qualifying income (for an 80 percent mortgage on homes selling at the median price) of close to triple that of the Houston resident. Clearly homes are not affordable in the New York Metropolitan Area.

HOUSING AFFORDABILITY AROUND THE COUNTRY

Figures are for the fourth quarter of 1988. The qualifying income is that needed to buy the median home, assuming an 80 percent mortgage at prevailing rates. Affordability is the ratio of median family income to qualifying income.

Metropolitan Area	Median Home Price	Qualifying Income	Median Family Income	Afford-ability
Houston	$ 65,800	$21,250	$37,059	1.74
Cleveland	70,600	22,800	39,438	1.73
Pittsburgh	63,700	20,572	35,036	1.70
Denver	79,700	25,739	38,497	1.50
St. Louis	75,700	24,447	35,468	1.45
Seattle	91,900	29,679	39,027	1.31
Chicago	101,400	32,747	41,520	1.27
Miami	82,900	26,772	31,419	1.17
Washington	129,700	41,886	46,700	1.11
Philadelphia	104,800	33,845	35,321	1.04
Boston	182,800	59,034	40,253	0.68
San Francisco	228,100	73,664	43,787	0.59
Los Angeles	191,200	61,747	36,406	0.59
New York	178,500	57,646	33,203	0.58
Honolulu	231,400	74,729	39,899	0.53

Source: *The New York Times*, March 18, 1989.

WHY THE EXPLOSION
IN HOME PRICES?

Several explanations are offered for the dramatic rise in real estate prices that has occurred in many regions of the country. One explanation is based on population trends. Beginning in the 1970s, the baby-boom generation came to be of home-buying age and the pressure of its numbers upon the housing market was one cause of the explosion of home prices during the late seventies and eighties.

Buyers themselves are given some of the blame for higher home prices. They want more house. A fireplace, for example, is increasingly asked for, as is central air conditioning.

Efforts on the part of local governments to slow growth in their communities—by zoning laws that set a minimum building lot size of two acres or more, for example—often limit housing supply and contribute to higher prices. Many local governments are now requiring builders of new housing developments to assume the costs of roads, parks, schools, and sewer hookups—costs which are passed along to home buyers.

Another reason for the high prices of today's new homes is that many builders who once geared their products to the first-time home buyer have turned from that market to the "trade-up" market. Home owners who bought their dwellings back in the low-price days are obviously enjoying a substantial increase in the value of those homes. Many sell and use the proceeds to buy bigger, more luxurious, better located homes. This "trading-up" is so prevalent that more than half the country's home builders are catering to the market for bigger, upscale homes. Mass production of modest homes, geared to the capacities of today's potential first-time buyers, now plays a very small part in the building industry.

The few builders who have chosen to stay with that market face overwhelming demand. One New Jersey builder, confronted with 14,772 responses to a newspaper ad offering houses in the $150,000 price range, resorted to a lottery to select the purchasers of his 250 homes.[4]

The highest-priced houses are along the east and west coasts, in cities and suburbs where strong business conditions and land shortage are cited as the major reasons for the price level. By comparison, one housing expert pointed out that in the Midwest the cities "can grow forever into the wheat fields." But in 1987 one-eighth-acre building lots in Orange County, California, were being offered at $80,000 and up. Empty lots!

High prices are not the only obstacle would-be home buyers have been confronting in recent years. There also has been some tightening of standards by mortgage lenders. In deciding whether to act favorably on a family's mortgage application, banks and other lenders consider what percentage of the family's income will be consumed by its monthly mortgage payments and other housing costs. Some banks that were willing to go along with housing costs that consume 33 percent of the family's income are now saying that 25 percent is the acceptable limit. Other banks are insisting that the source of the down payment must be the family's savings, not assistance from family or friends. What lies ahead?

FUTURE PROSPECTS FOR HOME BUYERS

Home price inflation has already started to cool and that cooling is expected to continue. Again, population trends

offer a demand/supply explanation. Between 1980 and 1987 more than 12 million new houses were built while only 8.7 million new households were formed.[5] Looking ahead, the 76 million baby boomers are being followed by the very much smaller "baby bust" generation born between 1965 and 1976. New household formation is expected to slow significantly in the years ahead and thus reduce demand for homes.

On the other hand, there is the huge pool of would-be home buyers who up to now have been priced out of the market. Their reentry, should prices cool further, could cushion a falling market.

The housing market may be about to work its way toward a solution to would-be home buyers' frustrations. But it is unlikely that the nation is going to sit still and wait for this to happen. "The middle income people are getting hammered," one building industry executive observed, and past experience indicates that middle-income people have political clout.

It has taken the national shame of homelessness to galvanize the public to think about the state of low-income housing but, as a recent headline in a major newspaper proclaimed: "Home Buying Is an Official Cause Again." Congress and state legislatures are trying to do something.

(Top) A sign advertises expensive homes for sale, while (bottom) the prohibitive pricing of homes for first-time buyers produces a sales glut in the suburban real estate market.

What kind of help is most needed by would-be first-time home buyers? In the opinion of some experts, help with the down payment for the home purchase is more crucial than reducing interest costs over a thirty-year mortgage term. A number of help-the-first-time-home-buyer legislative remedies are being proposed and the thrust of most of them is to help with the accumulation of funds for down payments. Employers too are initiating plans to help with down payments, and one expert predicts that "housing assistance will be the major new employee benefit of the 1990s."

A HIGHLY CONTROVERSIAL HOUSING ISSUE

As a wind-up for four chapters on households with housing problems, it will be interesting to give some thought to the top 15 percent of the nation's taxpayers who have absolutely no housing problems at all. In fact, we find to our amazement that they are receiving a housing subsidy from the federal government that dwarfs the subsidies embodied in public housing, rental assistance, and every other form of housing assistance. Incredible? Yes, but true. Here's how they get it.

John Doe owns a house. It is mortgaged. Last year the interest part of his mortgage payments was $3,580. He paid property taxes of $900. When he prepares his income tax return he subtracts those two figures (total $4,480) from his income before computing his tax. Assuming that the tax rate for his income is 25 percent, he saves $1,120 on his income tax by doing that subtraction. This is perfectly legal. The tax code and the income tax instructions tell him to do exactly what he did.

Now look at what John Doe did from the point of view of the federal government. By telling him that he may deduct his mortgage interest and his property taxes from his income before computing his income tax, the government has given up $1,120 in taxes that it could have otherwise received. This break for the taxpayer is called a *tax expenditure* because it has the same effect on the government's financial condition as if it had *spent* $1,120.

In 1986 the federal government's financial records showed receipts of about $769 billion. It is estimated that it would have taken in $37 billion more if home owners had not been permitted to take the two kinds of deductions that John Doe took. These Treasury Department estimates and the figures below suggest the disparity between the subsidy that results from tax expenditures related to housing and direct outlays for housing assistance.

	Tax Expenditures Related to Housing (billions)	Direct Outlays for Housing Assistance (billions)
1980	$28.8	$6.1
1981	35.3	7.4
1982	44.1	9.0

Source: Chester Hartman, ed., *America's Housing Crisis: What Is to Be Done?* The Institute for Policy Studies. (Boston: Routledge & Kegan Paul, 1983), p. 61.

Home owner deductions make up over 90 percent of the housing-related tax expenditures cited above and by far the largest home owner deductions are those for mortgage interest and property taxes.

It has long been assumed that the benefits that flowed from housing tax expenditures were sufficiently widespread and substantial to justify them. They were deemed an incentive to home ownership and a bulwark for the middle class.

However, recent studies such as those depicted in the graph below, have produced findings that question those assumptions. In the first place, only about 50 percent of home owners even use the deductions. Some have no taxable income; some find they fare better taking the standard deduction rather than itemizing their deductions. It was found that in 1981, for example, 80 percent of the tax benefit enjoyed through the two deductions went to the top 15 percent of the nation's taxpayers. It was, in other words, a housing subsidy to affluent home owners.[6]

Deduction of mortgage interest and property taxes is a sacred cow and to propose any modification of the

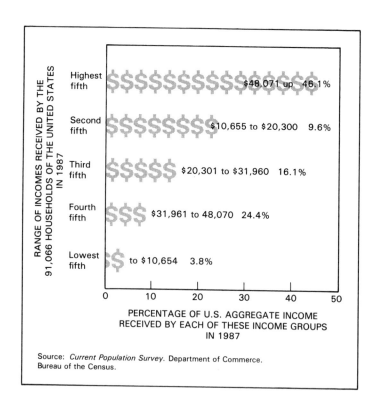

RANGE OF INCOMES RECEIVED BY THE 91,066 HOUSEHOLDS OF THE UNITED STATES IN 1987

Highest fifth $48,071 up 46.1%

Second fifth $10,655 to $20,300 9.6%

Third fifth $20,301 to $31,960 16.1%

Fourth fifth $31,961 to 48,070 24.4%

Lowest fifth to $10,654 3.8%

PERCENTAGE OF U.S. AGGREGATE INCOME RECEIVED BY EACH OF THESE INCOME GROUPS IN 1987

Source: *Current Population Survey.* Department of Commerce. Bureau of the Census.

privilege is politically hazardous. Actually, even those who feel most strongly about the inequity of the subsidy refrain from any suggestion that the practice be abolished. But in these days of budget deficits and urgent unmet social needs, it has become possible to talk about the hitherto unmentionable. It is not inconceivable that some legislative limit on these deductions might emerge.

CHAPTER SEVEN

LOW-INCOME HOUSING?
OF COURSE!
BUT NOT HERE

Six days a week Gary C. gets up at 4:00 A.M. and shortly thereafter leaves home for work. Home, for Gary, his wife, and daughter is an attractive two-bedroom condo in an outlying area of a New Jersey city. Gary will spend a long working day driving a delivery truck for a downtown florist, a job for which he is paid $23,000 a year. Three hours later Gary's next-door neighbor, Hal, leaves an identical condo for his downtown job as a junior executive, salary $65,000 a year.

Gary paid $46,000 for his condo just days after Hal had bought his for $140,000.

$\mathbf{G}$ARY is one of the 274 residents in the development who bought at below-market prices; Hal is one of the 972 who paid market price. The developer could easily have sold all 1,246 units at the higher price. Why didn't he? Because he was complying with the city's inclusionary zoning regulations. Inclusionary zoning, resulting from court decisions or legislation, is the emerging antidote to the exclusionary zoning that has produced income discrimination in housing.

EXCLUSIONARY ZONING
AND ITS EFFECTS

The power to regulate land use within its boundaries is usually delegated to local political units by state legislatures. How that power is used has enormous impact on the way a community develops.

The cost of a house includes the cost of the land on which it is built. Suppose two builders erect houses that cost, in labor and materials, $40,000. Builder A builds his in the part of a community where the zoning law requires 2-acre minimum building lots. Builder B builds his in an area where the law requires only half-acre lots. Obviously Builder A will have to put a higher price tag on his house than Builder B. Buyers who can buy in B's area can't buy in A's area.

In other words, a community can keep out low- and even moderate-income households by enacting zoning laws requiring large building plots. Such laws are referred to as exclusionary zoning. Take one Connecticut city, for example. Data from the 1980 census showed a median household income of $10,889 in the South End and a median household income of $51,957 in a northern part of the city, where land is zoned for one-, two-, and three-acre residences.

While the effect of exclusionary zoning is income discrimination, the rationale offered by communities that enact such legislation is much more benign, and often legitimately so. It may reflect a desire to curb population growth that would put pressure on community resources such as water or sewage, or on community services such as schools.

To achieve these slow-growth or no-growth ends, another heavily used zoning device is density regulations. Zoning an area for single-family dwellings only produces an entirely different effect from a regulation that permits the creation of multiple dwellings.

THE MOUNT LAUREL CASES

Once discrimination in housing became a public issue, it was inevitable that exclusionary zoning would be challenged in the courts. Mount Laurel, New Jersey, produced two landmark cases on income discrimination. In the first case, *So. Burlington County NAACP v. Township of Mount Laurel* (1975), the New Jersey Supreme Court ruled that each of New Jersey's 567 communities must provide zoning for low- and moderate-income households.

This ruling produced enormous amounts of pro and

con discussion, but no new affordable housing units. Developers simply said they couldn't afford to produce such units unless communities made zoning concessions that they just wouldn't make.

In a second exclusionary zoning lawsuit, *Mount Laurel II* (1983), the New Jersey Supreme Court reiterated its 1975 position, and then went on to say to the communities of New Jersey, in effect: Use the so-called "builders' remedy." Adjust your density and lot size regulations to accommodate any builder who says he will offer 20 percent of the units he builds at affordable prices. Allowing the builder to erect more units than you normally would will give him a high enough return so he can afford to sell a limited number of units at substantially lower prices.

In an attempt to take this whole matter out of the courts, the New Jersey legislature passed the 1985 Fair Housing Act, establishing a Council on Affordable Housing to implement the Mount Laurel doctrine.

The original intent of Mount Laurel had been that all the new low- and moderate-income units were to be placed in the suburbs. The Fair Housing Act modified the obligations of the suburbs by stating that of the 145,707 low- and moderate-income housing units to be produced by 1993—the goal set by the council—80,000 were to be in cities. The remainder were parcelled out, each suburb being assigned its quota, or "fair share." However, a suburb could enter into a contract with a neighboring city transferring half its quota of units to the city along with funds to cover the cost of producing those units.

It is estimated that some fourteen communities have moved to fulfill their Mount Laurel obligations. At least 10 transfers have been approved resulting in the production of about 800 low- and moderate-income housing units in New Jersey cities.

Mount Laurel accounts for Gary C.'s bargain condo. The city in which it is located had a zoning limitation of six condos per acre. A developer went in with a proposition to build fourteen condos per acre, eleven to sell at market levels and three below, and got what he asked for.

MOUNT LAUREL COMPLIANCE: AN UPHILL STRUGGLE

There has been substantial resistance to Mount Laurel and some criticism that the Council on Affordable Housing has not been sufficiently aggressive in forcing compliance. But one community's recent experience suggests that the council may be getting tougher.

Fanwood, a small suburb of Newark, was assigned eighty-seven units but claimed that its 1.2-square-mile area was already fully built up. There was no room for eighty-seven units. Then three developers offered proposals to demolish five single-family houses at three separate sites, empty houses which the developers had acquired. On those sites they would build sixty town houses, sell forty-eight at market rates and set aside twelve for sale at affordable prices to families with incomes under $27,200. Fanwood officials appealed to the council to permit them to turn down the developers' proposals. Residents of Fanwood and other communities that were offering the "no available land" excuse for doing nothing about low-income housing argued that if developers were allowed to demolish single-family homes to erect multi-family projects, whole neighborhoods could be destroyed. In this instance the council took a tough line with Fanwood officials: Come up with a plan for producing eighty-seven low-income units or let the developers go ahead with their plans. The "no land" tactic is out.

Many communities that are slow to comply with Mount Laurel just don't want low- and moderate-income housing. One New Jersey town—let's call it Rivertown—where available homes carry price tags of $400,000 to $1 million, was assigned a quota of 284 units. A builder who owns eight acres of land in the town proposed a development of eighty town houses, sixty-four to sell for $400,000 and sixteen at a subsidized, affordable price. Under the eligibility rules that determine who may buy the affordable units, a family of four with an income of $33,680 would be eligible in the county in which Rivertown is located. Rivertown's reaction to the proposal was expressed very forthrightly by the mayor: "that's not the kind of person they want in Rivertown. . . . I wouldn't want to see low- and moderate-income homes. It would decrease the value. If I wanted to move to Florida and sell my home, the big money wouldn't be there."

The Mount Laurel cases established a principle that has had significant impact on policy and practice outside New Jersey. But its achievements in terms of moving inner-city poor into superior, affordable, suburban housing have been limited. The relatively low-priced housing units that have become available as a result of Mount Laurel are still beyond the reach of that target population. Few can come up with the down payments, low as they are. Because of this, critics of Mount Laurel argue that future implementation efforts should give more emphasis to the production of rental units. Inner-city poor, they maintain, will always require government subsidies to become buyers of even very moderately priced homes.

Actually, the income limits that define who is eligible to buy Mount Laurel affordable units made them available to a very different group of buyers from those the courts had in mind. As of late 1988 the top of the range of qualifying incomes was $43,100 for a family of eight. Many young, upwardly mobile professionals, starting out at low salaries, were able to meet the income ceiling requirements and were quick to snatch up a substantial number of the limited housing units that were actually produced.

As of late 1988 it was estimated that only about 2,000 units of affordable housing had been produced and only 161 of New Jersey's 567 communities had submitted plans for producing their quotas of affordable housing.

INCLUSIONARY ZONING
THROUGH LEGISLATION

The courts brought inclusionary zoning to New Jersey. Legislation is introducing it elsewhere. The state of California not only requires that local governments provide for the housing needs of people of all income levels but also orders them to devise inducements that will encourage developers to produce low- and moderate-income housing.

Some of the local plans that have emerged in response to this legislation link office or other nonresidential construction with low-income housing. In San Francisco, builders of at least 50,000 square feet of office space have three options. They can build low-income housing themselves—nine-tenths of a housing unit for each 1,000 square feet of office space—they can finance the building or rehabilitation by others of that number of low-income units, or they can contribute to a housing trust fund that is used to subsidize the mortgages of low- and moderate-income families buying existing homes.

This linkage between business construction and low-income housing merits emphasis. Employers need employees so they have a stake in programs that provide

The Riverton housing complex in Harlem,
New York, is an example of public housing
subsidized by the private sector.

housing for them. States need businesses within their borders to build their tax base and provide employment for their residents. Companies have moved out of states because the housing situation created staffing problems. So it is understandable that active involvement of employers in low-income housing efforts is happening and is likely to intensify.

Massachusetts has passed, and Connecticut is trying to pass, inclusionary zoning legislation that works like this: If a developer submits a plan in which 20 percent of the units in his project will be set aside for low-income buyers, and the town rejects that plan, he can appeal to a land-use court. In that court the burden of proof will be on the town. The developer will not have to support his application. Rather, the town will have to offer hard evidence of damage that would be done to the town were his project to go through.

Inclusionary zoning is here to stay. The state housing commissioner of Connecticut was almost certainly prophetic when he argued this way for the proposed legislation mentioned above: "Let us not wait for someone—or something—else to tell us what we all know we must do."

Housing discrimination based on income is inextricably linked with discrimination on the basis of race. True, there are many more poor white people than poor black people. But the percentage of blacks who are poor is higher than the percentage of whites who are poor.[1] So when suburban communities shut out low-income people, when cities put all the low-income housing projects in one area, racial segregation is inevitably increased.

An example is the story that follows—the saga of Yonkers, New York.

CHAPTER EIGHT

FOR RENT/FOR SALE— BUT ONLY TO THE "RIGHT" PEOPLE

Mayor Nicholas C. Wasicsko, who had urged compliance with the judge's plan in order to halt the contempt-of-court fines that were doubling each day, said the crisis had hurt morale in the city. "People are holding their breath to see how the election comes out," he said.

The housing crisis is expected to dominate this year's election campaign, with challengers lining up on both sides of the housing issue.[1]

THE YONKERS story began in December 1980 as a school desegregation case brought by the U.S. Justice Department against the Yonkers school board and the Yonkers City Council. The school board, said the Justice Department, is guilty of deliberate discrimination because it has allowed Yonkers schools to become racially segregated. The charge then made an unprecedented linkage: the city government is also responsible for racial segregation in the schools because that segregation was the direct result of the city's public housing policies.

HOW THE CRISIS DEVELOPED

There was no question about the facts. Yonkers had placed all its public housing in the west side of the city. The public housing population was predominantly black. The student bodies of the schools in the west side were predominantly black.

In November 1985, U.S. District Judge Leonard Sand ruled that Yonkers had deliberately practiced racial discrimination over a period of forty years. Here, he ruled, is the remedial action that must be taken: (1) The

An aerial view of the city of
Yonkers, whose desegregation problems
have attracted nationwide debate.

city must build 200 units of low-income public housing on 7 east side, predominantly white, neighborhood sites. (2) The city must bring about the private development of 800 units of federally subsidized rental housing for families with incomes of between $15,000 and $32,000. These must be in the predominantly white north and east areas of the city.

The city council simply ignored Judge Sand's order for almost three years. Then in January 1988, faced with threats of staggering fines, the council accepted the order. It soon became clear, however, that acceptance was not what many people in Yonkers wanted. As public opposition mounted, the council members stalled. While agreeing to go ahead with the 200-unit requirement, they tried all kinds of tactics to get out of the second part of what Judge Sand considered an accepted agreement. In June the judge ordered the council to pass the zoning and other legislation needed to get started on the 800 units in the required locations. By a vote of 4 to 3 the council refused to do so.

Thereupon Judge Sand held the council members in contempt of court and imposed impressive penalties: fines of $500 per day on individual council members plus the assurance that jail sentences were imminent; and fines on the city that started at $100 and doubled daily.

Public opinion, whipped into a frenzy by a video-tape of squalid conditions in one housing project, warmly supported the council's vote. The vice-mayor's assertion that he would "go to jail for twenty years if I have to" made him a public hero. But when an appeal to the Supreme Court to delay the fines failed, the city's financial situation soon became precarious. A state panel appointed to monitor the situation talked of freezing wages and ordering the dismissal of about one-fourth of the city's employees. With defeat inevitable, a major citizens' group that had backed the council's defiance urged its members to yield. Two members of the council changed their votes on compliance from "no" to "yes," so Yonkers seemed committed to do exactly what Judge Sand ordered it to do.

The vote to comply freed Yonkers from the financial penalties it had been incurring, but it produced no real progress toward the production of the 800 housing units. In the primary elections of September 1989, genuine compliance with the court's rulings was clearly an issue. Mayor Nicholas Wasicsko easily won renomination in the Democratic primary over an opponent who opposed compliance. But whether compliance or resistance supporters will have a majority on the city council after the November election is an open question as this book goes to press.

A NEW PRINCIPLE FROM THE HUNTINGTON CASE

In November 1988, Huntington, Long Island, was the site of another major ruling on racial discrimination in housing, this time a decision of the U.S. Supreme Court.

The town of Huntington includes in its almost 100-square-mile area some of Long Island's wealthiest and poorest areas, ranging from a section dotted with million-dollar waterfront mansions to a section dominated by low-income housing developments. The section of the town in which this low-income housing is located is, under Huntington's zoning statute, the only part of the town in which apartments can be built. Huntington's population is predominantly white but the section in which the low-income housing is located is predominantly black.

Housing Help Inc., a nonprofit housing group, applied to the town for a variance to build 162 garden apartments in a predominantly white area zoned for single-family homes. The application was turned down and Housing Help took the matter to court. When the case came before the federal courts, the Court of Appeals for the Second Circuit ruled in favor of Housing Help. It ordered Huntington to rezone 14.8 acres, in the area designated by Housing Help, to permit construction of 162 apartments for low-income families.

In explaining its ruling, the court cited a mid-1980s survey carried out by the town. That survey had established that 24 percent of Huntington's approximately 10,000 black families needed subsidized housing while only 7 percent of the total town population of about 200,000 needed such housing.[2] Inevitably, therefore, said the court, when the zoning law caused all the town's subsidized housing to be placed in one area, that area would become a black, segregated area. The fact that segregation was not the *intent* of the town's zoning law is immaterial, said the court. The law had the *effect* of promoting segregation and is therefore in violation of the federal 1968 Fair Housing Act.

When the town appealed the case to the Supreme Court, the higher tribunal refused to overturn the lower court's ruling, thus affirming the principle embodied in the ruling. Obviously this is a principle that could be invoked in other communities, and probably will be.

In light of the Huntington case, it is interesting to note that HUD's rules governing site selection for public housing projects now limit the number of subsidized housing units that can be placed near existing concentrations of poor households.

INDIVIDUALS ON THE FIRING LINE

Thus far in this chapter, as in the preceding chapter, the focus has been on examples of and remedies for discrimination against groups of people. Equally in need of redress are acts of discrimination against individuals that can only be remedied on a case by case basis.

Take the case of Theron and Claire C. They were highly paid black professionals seeking an apartment. Prepared to pay $1,200 a month for a two-bedroom apartment, they knew that the predominantly white areas they had chosen to explore were well within their rental budget. But real estate offices in those areas said nothing was available; vacancies listed in newspapers turned out to be "taken."

A number of studies have tried to determine how prevalent discrimination is in real estate offices. Black and white "testers" visit the same agents, ask for the same type of housing, and give similar employment and financial data. Every such study reveals a pattern: black and other minority home seekers are denied access to housing that is readily offered to whites.

This pattern prevails despite the fact that such practices have been illegal for over thirty years. Some lawsuits are brought, some fines are paid, the occasional real estate license is temporarily suspended. But discrimination persists.

One new approach, however, has led to happy endings for some minority apartment seekers. A few lawsuits brought against owners by an open housing advocacy group have resulted in agreements been the two parties. Landlords have promised to rent every third or fourth future vacancy in their buildings to qualified applicants provided by the agency.

REDLINING

A number of studies have found another kind of housing discrimination against minorities—discrimination in the mortgage market. The table on page 107 shows how a minority applicant who applies for a mortgage on a house in a predominantly minority neighborhood is much less likely to be approved than a white applicant buying a home in a white neighborhood, even though the financial qualifications of the two applicants are equal. In other words, lending institutions engage in *redlining*—refusal to lend in low-income minority neighborhoods.

BLACK AND WHITE DISPARITIES
Ten metro areas with the highest ratio of black-to-white loan rejections

	Black rejection rate	White rejection rate	Black-white rejection ratio
Milwaukee	24.2%	6.2%	3.90:1
Pittsburgh	31.2%	8.2%	3.80:1
Cleveland	31.4%	8.4%	3.74:1
Chicago	27.6%	7.6%	3.63:1
Detroit	32.5%	9.1%	3.57:1
Norfolk Virginia Beach Newport News Charlotte	26.5%	7.7%	3.44:1
Gastonia, N.C. Rock Hill, S.C.	26.1%	8.0%	3.26:1
Indianapolis	27.9%	8.7%	3.21:1
Baltimore	24.2%	7.6%	3.18:1
Memphis Ark.-Miss.	22.2%	7.3%	3.04:1
U.S. average	23.7%	11.1%	2.14:1

Source: *U.S. News & World Report*, February 27, 1989, p. 26.

This kind of discrimination is illegal. The 1977 Community Reinvestment Act states that banks must make loans to *all* the neighborhoods within the area they serve. While enforcement of the law has been very lax, there has been some increase in the amount of mortgage funds made available to minority borrowers. In a few places banks have gotten together with community groups and agreed upon the percentage of their lending that would go to neighborhoods previously not well served.

ANOTHER WAY OUT
OF THE PROJECTS

The last program to be described is an individualized, case-by-case remedy for the group segregation that so often characterizes public housing. Listen to Victoria R., one of its beneficiaries. "In the city I got a cousin strung out on cocaine and a niece who will be pregnant before she's eleven. My kids, they don't know about these things. Out here, all they need to know is they can grow up to be a doctor or a lawyer." The city Victoria R. is talking about is Chicago. "Out here" is a nearly all-white suburb of Chicago where she and her two children now live in a three-bedroom rent-subsidized apartment in a privately owned building.

To get there, she waited her turn on a list of 2,000 families. Then she survived a screening process that included an evaluation of her credit standing, a check for a possible criminal record, and scrutiny of her house-keeping practices. After the screening came counseling aimed at preparing her to cope with the ways of suburbia.

Victoria R.'s family is one of about 3,500 families, most headed by single mothers, that have been rehoused under a HUD-funded program run by a Chicago fair-housing group. Some of the families were moved into predominantly white areas of the city; more than half were scattered among 118 suburbs, the wide scattering a deliberate attempt to avoid stirring up opposition. Neighbors know the new arrivals are different, but they do not know about the public housing background and rent subsidies.

This Chicago program stemmed from a judge's order deciding a case initiated on behalf of Dorothy Gautreaux and several other public housing tenants. These plaintiffs argued that the Chicago Housing Authority's practice of building all public housing in black neighborhoods was racial discrimination.

Has the program worked? There has been a cross-burning and some racial epithets scrawled on walls, but also reports of acceptance and friendliness. Only 10 percent of the families moved out of the city are believed to have given up and moved back. Clearly recognized as beneficiaries are the children, whose educational prospects have been so vastly improved in their new suburban schools.

NO CHILDREN!

To introduce another kind of discrimination, listen to Shamee G. testifying before a Congressional committee about her inability to use her Section 8 certificate: "I take the papers and I go through the want ad [sic]. And I call every house. Every house. They don't want Section 8 or they don't want kids. My Section 8 is going to be running out soon."

Discrimination against families with children is rampant, as is discrimination against single-parent fam-

Philadelphia resident Tamara Fletcher (left)
was one of twelve low-income families selected
to live in two historic rowhouses renovated
by the city government in conjunction with
private corporations and non-profit groups.

ilies. One 1987 estimate placed the number of minority single-parent families who were unable to use rent vouchers in big cities at 75 percent.[3]

TOWARD A MORE EFFECTIVE
FAIR HOUSING ACT

Open housing advocates have high hopes that the 1988 changes in the Fair Housing Act will make substantial inroads against discrimination. In the first place, the changes broadened the scope of the law to cover disabled persons and families with children.

Second, the enforcement process was strengthened. Hitherto, persons who claimed to have been victims of discrimination could complain to HUD. HUD's role was to investigate complaints and try to mediate between the parties or effect out-of-court settlements. If those attempts were unsuccessful, the offended persons had to initiate their own lawsuits. Under the amended act, government lawyers will handle the cases of those who file complaints, taking the cases to court if necessary. Fines for discrimination offenses were made much higher, especially for repeat offenders.

SUCCESS DESPITE
DISCRIMINATION

It would be misleading not to remind readers at this point that despite the obstacles cited above, thousands of minority renters and home buyers have successfully moved on their own into buildings and communities that once were closed to them. Ironically, that very success has had an unfavorable impact, some claim, upon those left behind. The exodus of middle-class business people and

Graffiti denouncing public housing
for blacks mar a housing project
construction site in New Jersey.

professionals from the city areas they once shared with less successful minority members has, it is said, meant a loss of needed role models and a weakening of some of the social constraints that gave cohesion and stability to inner-city communities.

CHAPTER NINE

HOUSING'S
THOUSAND POINTS
OF LIGHT

Then I said to them, "You see the trouble we are in,
how Jerusalem lies in ruins with its gates burned.
Come, let us build the wall of Jerusalem, that we may
no longer suffer disgrace. . . ." And they said, "Let
us rise up and build."   Nehemiah 2:17–18

IN THE LATE 1970s, fifty-two Brooklyn churches, concerned by the urgent need for affordable housing in distressed areas of Brooklyn, joined together and said: "Let us build homes for people who need them." As a result of that declaration of purpose, on October 31, 1982 ground was broken, on a 30-square-block site, for a three-bedroom town house. Taking advantage of the economies that can be achieved by building a large number of similar houses in a compact area, the contractors completed that house and 1,049 just like it. They were sold at prices ranging from $39,000 to $47,500 and are now homes for families that earn no more than $20,000 a year.

The city of New York gave the land to the church group that sponsored the project. The churches provided the builders with $12 million of zero-interest construction loans. Buyers who needed help with down payments found $10,000 loans available from the city along with a promise of no property taxes for ten years. The state offered low-interest mortgage loans.

Mindful of the fact that the prophet Nehemiah had brought about the rebuilding of the walls of Jerusalem, the sponsors of this new way of making low-income families home owners named the program the Nehemiah

Plan. Fifty-three hundred families are on a waiting list for more Nehemiah Plan houses.

A WIDENING ROLE
FOR STATES

The Nehemiah Plan was chosen to open this chapter for a specific reason. The federal government had no part in it. Thus it is an appropriate introduction to a chapter whose purpose is to show how others have moved into housing activity as the withdrawal of the federal government created an unacceptable vacuum.

As an essential response to the federal government's vastly reduced housing assistance during the 1980s, the states have greatly increased the extent and diversity of their efforts to provide affordable housing for low- and moderate-income families. Traditionally, states have raised funds for housing through the sale of tax-free bonds. Now, in addition to that source, they are budgeting for varied housing programs from their general revenues; they are devoting to housing purposes such diverse funds as offshore oil revenues, casino tax revenues, lawsuit settlement proceeds, and pension funds.

To accomplish housing goals states are joining with municipalities, counties, foundations, churches, hospitals, universities, nonprofit housing corporations, banks, developers, and a wide variety of partnerships of those entities. They offer below-market-rate first mortgages, second mortgages, loan guarantees, rent-payment guarantees, and direct subsidies. And they are a funding source for many initiatives undertaken by their local communities.

Particularly ingenious have been states' efforts to provide for those who have special housing needs: group homes for the handicapped, single-room occupancy structures, apartments with child-care services, house-sharing programs.

Many states have responded to the special needs of the elderly. Under so-called congregate housing programs, facilities are built that enable senior citizens who have no need for supervision or intensive health care to live in their own apartments, eating meals that are prepared in a central kitchen, either in their own apartments or, more often, in a central dining room.

SOME HOUSING
INITIATIVES BY CITIES

Cities too have broadened their housing efforts and produced some promising new approaches to housing problems. Take San Diego, California. The 207-room Baltic Inn opened in 1987, a creative response to an acute housing need—decent, affordable housing for low-income individuals. In a typical 10- by 15-foot carpeted room is a double bed, color television, microwave oven, small refrigerator, and a toilet separated by a small partition. Showers are down the hall. Rent is $80 a week, lower on a monthly basis. To build this kind of housing at a cost of $20,000 a room, a cost level essential if affordable rates were to be charged, the city had to relax some of the stringent rules in its building codes.

Not intended for the poorest of the poor, the Baltic Inn represents a San Diego experiment in housing for the clientele that once used the old SRO hotels, until urban renewal and other face-lifting programs swept so many of them away.

Athens, Tennessee. City officials approached the residents of a deteriorating area with this proposition: If

you will pay for the needed materials, we will supply the labor—carpenters, plumbers, painters, electricians, and so forth—to fix up your homes. Banks cooperated to the extent of offering low-interest loans to householders who took advantage of the city's proposal.

New York City. A Housing Partnership helps varied combinations of community groups, banks, and builders put together all the ingredients needed to build houses and finance their sale to low- and moderate-income buyers. As of the end of 1988 they had helped to produce 2,500 houses in 35 different locations and had plans in the works for 2,000 more on 25 other sites.

The typical buyer of the kind of homes they sponsor—initially their average price was $75,000—has about $10,000 to get started on home ownership. With closing costs of about $4,000 to be covered, the remaining $6,000 is not enough for a 10 percent down payment on a $75,000 house. A 95 percent mortgage covers the situation, but mortgages at that level are relatively scarce. The Housing Partnership was able to bring another entity into the picture—a city employees' pension fund that agreed to permit part of the funds it was putting into

The city of Providence, Rhode Island, is rehabilitating this three-decker apartment house through its Stop Wasting Abandoned Property program, designed to provide low-income housing to the city's residents.

housing to be used for 95 percent mortgages on projects under Housing Partnership auspices.

Baltimore, Maryland. One recent September day a private contractor's workmen began tearing out the interiors of nine buildings that had been abandoned by the owners, taken over by the city, and donated to the contractor. His commitment was to create low-cost homes. Once the buildings were reduced to empty shells without roofs, on November 10 a crane began dropping in factory-built floors of rooms, complete with plumbing and carpeting. Two weeks later, the first family moved in. A local builder commented: "Is modular housing the magic solution? No, but when combined with subsidies and help on the financing, it does offer a way for groups without the expertise to put up housing quickly."

Boston, Massachusetts. In 1953 a 48-acre, 30-building, 1,502-unit public housing project opened on an isolated waterfront site that had been a dump. By the late 1960s the project had become so horrendous that the vacancy rate approached 65 percent despite a serious housing shortage in the city.

Bad as the project was, the site was potentially attractive—an arm of land jutting into the harbor. In fact, gentrification of the area loomed. The families who had stuck it out in the project knew gentrification would mean demolition of the public housing project and no homes for them. Somehow they got the right officials to listen to their plight and a series of negotiations followed, far too technical and complicated to recount.

The outcome was that the whole area is being re-planned as a mixed-income community of 1,283 rental units. One-third of the original public housing buildings will be retained, but completely gutted and redesigned. The new buildings will be a mix of townhouses and mid-rise buildings up to seven stories. Tennis and basketball courts, a waterside park, a clinic, a day-care center, and retail space are part of the site plan, and tree-lined streets will tie it all together.

The 355 survivor families will move into apartments reserved for them, at rents a fraction of the market rate. Another group of apartments will be reserved for slightly higher income tenants who will need some subsidy, and the rest of the units will be offered at market rents.

The federal government had to play a part in this undertaking because a public housing project was involved, but it was totally a city initiative.

CITIES HELPING
PEOPLE BUY HOUSING

Many cities have *homesteading* programs. In homesteading, families are given the opportunity to pay part of the cost of buying a rehabilitated house or an apartment in a rehabilitated building by doing some of the rehabilitation work themselves. Paying for a home with one's labor rather than cash—so-called *sweat equity*— has worked well in many places, but it presents serious problems of supervision and management.

One city found a way to create a pool of mortgage money that could be offered at lower than prevailing market rates. It raised a substantial sum of money by the sale of tax-exempt bonds, then turned that fund over to a trustee. The trustee enlisted fourteen banks who agreed to dispense the money allocated by the trustee to borrowers seeking mortgage loans, permitting down payments of only 5 percent and offering below-market interest rates.

REHABILITATION EVERYWHERE

The most exciting thing about the stories of rehabilitation efforts around the country is their variety. Basically, of course, the stories are all the same: an abandoned house, or apartment house, or row of houses is taken over by a private builder, a nonprofit corporation, a community development group, a church, a union—whatever—and made into livable housing space.

One group of tenants abandoned by their landlord was guided by a community service society, and given financial help by two different local sources. The group did such a good job restoring essential services in their building and making it habitable that the landlord tried to reclaim the building. With the help of their friends the group fought off that threat and they now own their building.

(Top) In this example of homesteading, friends help a group of eight single parents renovate a building they had leased from the city. (Bottom) Maria Santana poses in the dining room of a house that her family occupied as squatters, rehabilitated, and now own outright in Philadelphia.

Elsewhere, a large-scale rehabilitation effort reached the stage where large amounts of debris had to be removed from the site. An organization that works with men newly released from prison, enlisted by the coordinator of the project, sent over crews of its clients to do the job. It was an interesting example of a human rehabilitation program contributing to a housing rehabilitation program.

New York City's rehabilitation plans must be reported simply because they are so vast. New apartments are to be created in no fewer than 47,000 abandoned buildings that are, in their present state, simply foundations and exterior walls. Some have been sold to private developers for $1 each, some to nonprofit groups. The city is retaining ownership of some and hiring contractors to do the renovations. Whoever buys the buildings, rehabilitates them. Buyers must put up 10 percent of the estimated rehabilitation cost, and the rest of the needed funds come partly from one-percent interest loans from the city and partly from market-rate loans from banks that have organized a special consortium to handle this financing. By 1993, homes for 250,000 families are to be created.

Business is deeply involved in rehabilitation. That involvement is particularly valuable when pooled business contributions provide a fund of sufficient magnitude to serve as backing or guarantor for small organizations seeking to achieve housing purposes. The Local Initiatives Support Corp. (LISC), for example, was founded by a major, wealthy, private foundation in 1980. It raises money from corporations and foundations to serve as seed money to attract other financing. Typical of its role is the Homesight project in Washington, D.C. LISC gave neighborhood development groups funds to buy from the city houses that had been seized for nonpayment of taxes. To rehabilitate them, the groups were able to borrow 80 percent of the rehabilitation costs from local banks at market rates because LISC guaranteed the groups' credit. The remaining 20 percent needed was covered by a LISC loan at a below-market rate. As a result, 125 renovated houses were available for sale at about $50,000 each.

There is, however, a downside to the rehabilitation story. Many projects are reported in which tenants of a run-down building undertake to rehabilitate it themselves and then manage it or convert it to a cooperative. Sometimes they work out well but often they do not. So many things go wrong; so many starts do not come to completion. It is an exciting idea for people to do with their own hands the work of improving their dwellings, especially so if they would otherwise be unemployed. But many simply do not have the needed skills; or, if they have skills their work is slower than that of experienced craftsmen. And they require intensive supervision.

Sponsoring community groups get into disagreements with developers that cause delays or even abandonment of projects. Even highly motivated volunteers turn out to be ill-equipped to handle the complexities of rehabilitating and restructuring the running of a building. And all tenants are just simply not capable of taking control or of working with others to achieve control or ownership.

A FINAL WORD OF CAUTION

In 1984 HUD issued a report entitled *Working Partners: 100 Success Stories of Local Community Development Public/Private Partnerships at Work.* Among the success stories are those of a new park in a public housing project in Leesburg, Virginia; 200 rehabilitated rental units in Burlington, Vermont; urban homesteading in Bayamon, Puerto Rico; a new apartment house in Durham, North Carolina, for families displaced by an expressway; home rehabilitation as part of a flood recovery program in Nebraska; Adventure Island, a special playground for handicapped children in Pascagoula, Mississippi; a closed-down chair factory converted to 120 spacious apartments for the elderly in Monroe, Michigan; an emergency shelter for the homeless created from an unused church rectory in Stamford, Connecticut.

The sites of the 100 stories are different; the projects are different. But a basic formula persists: a need is recognized and people of good will do something about it by pulling together the public and private agencies whose cooperative effort can meet the need. These stories carry another message, however. The federal government is very often needed in the partnership.

The success of all 100 stories hinged on federal money in the form of a Block Grant. (The Community Development Block Grant program is one of the channels through which federal funds are dispensed to localities for varied purposes, including housing.) Sometimes a large sum dominated the financing of the project, sometimes a modest amount gave the sponsors leverage to get more from other sources; millions or hundreds of thousands, the federal money was crucial.

Maybe all those 100 projects could have been carried out without a cent of federal money. After all, the whole purpose of this final chapter has been to demonstrate the amazing accomplishments of states and communities without federal help.

But knowledgeable people assure us that when programs like the federal Block Grants are cut back, forward movement at the local level on housing and other community improvement efforts is slowed down, or reduced to a scale inadequate to meet needs. (Obviously public housing and significant rental assistance programs can only happen with federal involvement.)

This, then, must be the message of this final chapter on the achievements of states and communities on their own: The enhanced role of local governments, state governments, nonprofit groups, social service organizations, unions, businesses, religious groups, coordinating entities that have been described, fruitful and promising as it is, must not be taken to add up to the answer to the nation's housing problems.

Their initiatives and successes must be viewed as evidence of the genius of our federal system, which provides fifty social laboratories in which to try diverse approaches to common problems. Their achievements and successes must not be interpreted to mean that the diminished role the federal government has chosen to play in recent years is acceptable. Housing experts are unanimous on that point.

They urge that some of the innovative state programs that have been initiated should be models for federal programs that will supersede them, that some local and state programs should remain local and state efforts but with new infusions of federal funds. They urge a coherent national housing policy and funding adequate for its implementation.

The very magnitude of the housing task mandates that the federal government, with its unique powers of taxing, allocation, and enforcement be involved. How many times have waiting lists been mentioned in descriptions of current housing programs? How many times has the use of the term lottery been justified? Not enough was done even in the years of less niggardly federal funding.

There is a promise on the books, an unfulfilled promise that is over forty years old. If every American family is to have "a decent home and a suitable living environment" the federal government will have to expand, not freeze or further reduce its commitment to housing. The vanguard of housing activists that has emerged in the last few years will have to take on the responsibility for seeing that that happens.

SOURCE NOTES

CHAPTER ONE

1. Jon Erickson and Charles Wilhelm, eds., *Housing the Homeless*, Center for Urban Policy Research (New Brunswick, N.J.: Rutgers University Press, 1986), 26.
2. Cited in Elizabeth Ehrlich, "Homelessness: the Policy Failure Haunting America," *Business Week*, 25 April 1988.
3. Ibid.
4. Ibid.
5. Jonathan Kozol, *Rachel and Her Children: Homeless Families in America* (New York: Crown, 1988), 206, 210.
6. Richard D. Bingham, Roy E. Green, and Sammis B. White, eds., *The Homeless in Contemporary Society* (Newbury Park, Cal.: Sage Publications, Inc., 1987), 221.
7. Kozol, op. cit., 208.
8. Nancy Amidei, "A Needless Shortage," *Commonweal*, 28 February 1986, 101.

CHAPTER TWO

1. " 'Families' Share of Households Has Shrunk," *The New York Times*, 22 September 1988, C8.
2. Martin Tolchin, "Minority Poverty on Rise But White Poor Decline," *The New York Times*, 1 September 1988.
3. Nora Richter Greer, *The Search for Shelter* (Washington, D.C.: The American Institute of Architects, 1986), 5.
4. Peter D. Salins, ed., *Housing America's Poor* (Chapel Hill: University of North Carolina Press, 1987), chapter 5.
5. Greer, op. cit.

CHAPTER THREE

1. David C. Anderson, "The Editorial Notebook: From the Outside: Yonkers II," *The New York Times,* 12 October 1988, A30.
2. Robert Kuttner, "Bad Housekeeping: the housing crisis and what to do about it," *New Republic,* 25 April 1988, 23.
3. William Julius Wilson, *The Truly Disadvantaged* (Chicago: University of Chicago Press, 1987), 25–26, 38.

CHAPTER FOUR

1. U.S. Congress. *The Assisted Housing Stock: Potential Losses from Prepayment and "Opt-Outs."* Report prepared by Congressional Research Service, No. 87-879E, 4 November 1987, 3.
2. Salins, op. cit.
3. David C. Schwartz, Richard C. Ferlauto, and Daniel N. Hoffman, *A New Housing Policy for America: Recapturing the American Dream* (Philadelphia: Temple University Press, 1988), 57.
4. *A Decent Place to Live: The Report of the National Housing Task Force,* March 1988, 6.

CHAPTER FIVE

1. Kuttner, op. cit., p. 22.
2. Robert Kuttner, "A Blueprint for Affordable Housing," *Business Week,* 31 August 1987, 18.
3. M. Bruce Johnson, ed., *Resolving the Housing Crisis,* Pacific Institute for Public Policy Research (Cambridge, Mass.: Ballinger Publishing Co., 1982), 283.
4. *A Decent Place to Live,* p. 7.
5. Salins, op. cit., 3.
6. "100 Million Places to Live," *The New York Times,* 29 March 1987, E5.
7. "42 Years of Rent Curbs Foster Inequities Among Tenants in New York City," *The New York Times,* 3 June 1985.
8. Anthony de Palma, "Landlords Are Trying a New Tack in Their Push for Deregulation," *The New York Times,* 13 March 1988, E6.

CHAPTER SIX

1. "Affording the unaffordable," *U.S. News & World Report,* 19 September 1988, 62.
2. Richard Eisenberg, "The New Vise on the Middle Class," *Money,* September 1987, 48.

3. Eisenberg, op. cit., 49.
4. Ibid.
5. Kenneth R. Sheets with Robert F. Black, "A roof, but no shelter," *U.S. News & World Report,* 8 March 1989, 47.
6. Salins, op. cit., 165.

CHAPTER SEVEN

1. Tolchin, op. cit.

CHAPTER EIGHT

1. James Feron, "Yonkers Moves Past Housing Battle," *The New York Times,* 11 February 1989, 30.
2. Eric Schmitt, "L.I. Town, Focus on Housing Bias Ruling, Reflects Many in the New York Region," *The New York Times,* 8 November 1988, B4.
3. Robert Kuttner, "Bad Housekeeping: the housing crisis and what to do about it," *New Republic,* 25 April 1988, 24.

GLOSSARY

Adjusted Income: The income figure used to determine eligibility for public housing and/or housing subsidies. It is computed by deducting from total income whatever allowances are specified in the area's housing regulations, such as deductions for children and elderly or handicapped household members.

Affordability Index: A measure of the relationship between the median income of households in an area and the qualifying income needed to purchase a home at the then-prevailing median price in that area. When the index is above 100, houses are deemed to be affordable because median income exceeds the qualifying income needed to purchase a home at the prevailing median price; an index number below 100 signals a tight housing market.

Amortization: The extinguishing of a debt, usually by prescribed periodic payments.

Appropriation: In the federal legislative process, an appropriation bill sets the amounts that the Treasury may pay out for specific projects during specific time periods.

Authorization: In the federal legislative process, an authorization bill empowers a government agency to enter upon or continue a specific project and sets the amount that it will be permitted to spend therefor.

Baby-boom Generation: The cohort of individuals born between 1946 and 1964.

Block Grant: Federal funds given to a local government unit under the Community Development Block Grant program which the local government may use for the achievement of any one of a wide variety of permissible community-improvement projects, including housing.

Bonds: Promises-to-pay given by governments or corporations to investors who lend them money. A bond specifies when the loan it represents will be repaid and how much interest will be paid during the loan period.

Certificate of Family Participation (Section 8 renter's certificate): A guarantee issued by HUD to a household to show to landlords, assuring landlords that a rent subsidy will be paid by HUD for that household.

Congregate Housing: Housing, primarily for senior citizens, that combines individual dwelling units with central dining/recreational areas.

Consortium: A group of banks—or other entities—joined together to accomplish a specific common objective.

Conventional Mortgage: A mortgage negotiated through the banking system, involving no government guarantee.

Entitlement Program: An assistance program in which any applicant who meets the legislatively mandated qualifications is entitled to receive the defined benefit.

Exclusionary Zoning: Land-use regulations that have the effect of keeping unwanted types of housing units out of the area covered by the regulations.

Fair Market Rents: The return builders are entitled to receive on rental units covered by Section 8 programs. They are computed to cover the builders' construction and operating costs.

Family: At least two persons related through birth, adoption, or marriage.

Filtering: The process by which housing units become available, over time, to progressively lower-income families.

Foreclosure: The seizure of property for failure to meet the obligations of a mortgage on that property.

Gentrification: The upgrading that takes place in a depressed, low-income neighborhood when middle- and/or upper-income families buy and rehabilitate run-down housing units in the area.

Homesteading: Housing programs that permit buyers to cover part of the cost of a rehabilitated housing unit by working on the rehabilitation.

Household: One or more persons occupying a housing unit.

House Sharing: Programs designed to bring together as joint occupants home owners who are having difficulty meeting their expenses as property owners and compatible individuals and/or families in need of housing.

Inclusionary Zoning: Land-use regulations designed to ensure that low- and moderate-income housing, not just upper-income housing, are constructed in the area covered by the regulations.

Lower-income Families: The term used by HUD to designate families in a specific area whose incomes are 50 to 80 percent of the median family income of that area.

Low-income Families: The term used by HUD to designate families in a specific area whose incomes are below 50 percent of the median family income of that area.

Market Rents: The rent levels that result from interaction between the supply of and the demand for rental housing in an area.

Median Family Income: The midpoint in the range of family incomes in a specifically defined area. Half the families of the area have incomes below the median, half above.

Modular Housing: Factory-produced housing building blocks—sections of a dwelling—put together into a housing unit on a home site.

Moratorium: A time period during which a specific activity is not required or not permitted.

Mortgage: A document giving a lender the right to claim a piece of property if the owner of that property fails to repay money borrowed from the mortgage holder.

Mortgage Insurance: A means of protecting lenders who hold mortgages, thus making lending for housing construction more attractive. If a borrower fails to meet his mortgage obligation the mortgage-insuring agency pays off the mortgage, thus saving the lender from the risk of loss if he had to take over the mortgaged property and sell it to recover his money.

Payment Standard: The term used in the voucher program to designate the amount a landlord is entitled to receive for a housing unit; it is always the same as the fair market rent prescribed by HUD for comparable units in the Section 8 program.

Poor: Having an income below the poverty level.

Poverty: The condition of being poor.

Poverty Levels: The minimum income levels required for families of varied sizes and composition to maintain adequate diets and meet other basic needs.

Productivity: Output per work-hour.

Public Housing Authority: An agency established by a state or local government to initiate and/or administer government sponsored housing activities in the area of its jurisdiction.

Qualifying Income: The income needed to meet the obligations of a mortgage of a specific amount and term.

Redlining: The illegal banking practice of refusing to lend for the purchase of property in low-income and/or minority-dominated areas.

Rent Control: A system under which a government agency sets the timing, the circumstances, and the size of permissible rent increases.

Section 8 Certificates: Guarantees granted by HUD to builders assuring them that they will receive subsidies to supplement tenants' rents for covered housing units, subsidies large enough for each covered unit to yield a fair market rent.

Seed Money: An initial investment in a project that demonstrates its feasibility or money-making potential and thus attracts further financing.

SRO: Residential buildings comprised of single-room housing units.

Subsidized Housing: Housing whose construction costs and/or operating expenses are partially covered by grants from government units or other sponsoring agencies.

Subsidized Mortgages: A device to encourage building construction by lowering the cost of mortgage borrowing. The borrower pays an interest rate lower than the going market rate and the government, or other subsidizing agency, makes up the difference to the lender.

Substandard Housing: Housing units that fail to meet HUD standards for equipment (kitchens and bathrooms), basic systems (heating, lighting), and maintenance (timely repairs and upkeep).

Sweat Equity: The partial ownership claim on a housing unit that is earned by the buyer's work on the unit.

Tax-exempt Bonds: Bonds whose interest need not be included in computing taxable income.

Tax Expenditure: A reduction in government revenue that results from a provision in the tax code that reduces the amounts that taxpayers are obligated to pay.

Tenement: Literally, any apartment building, but more generally used to designate substandard multiple dwellings in the poorer, crowded sections of urban areas.

Trading Up: The practice of selling one housing unit and using the proceeds for a more expensive housing unit.

Urban Renewal: The process of restoring the viability of physically and economically declining areas of a city.

Variance: An exception to a zoning regulation granted to a builder by a zoning authority.

Voucher: A guarantee issued by HUD to a household, assuring landlords that a rent subsidy will be paid by HUD for that household.

Warehousing: The withholding of rental units from the market, usually practiced by landlords moving toward the conversion of rental buildings to co-ops.

Zoning Laws: Legislation controlling land use within a specific area.

SUGGESTED READING LIST

A basic resource:

Jacobs, Barry G., Kenneth R. Harney, Charles L. Edson, Bruce S. Lane. *Guide to Federal Housing Programs*. Second Edition. Washington, D.C.: The Bureau of National Affairs, Inc., 1986.
(Not easy reading, but the most accessible, comprehensive presentation of past and present U.S. housing legislation.)

The most recent survey of the state of the nation's housing:

National Housing Task Force. *A Decent Place to Live: The Report of the National Housing Task Force*. March 1988. (As of 1988 copies were available from the Task Force staff at 1625 Eye Street, N.W., Suite 1015, Washington, D.C. 20006.)
(A readable presentation of the present housing picture in the United States, followed by detailed recommendations for achieving the nation's housing goals. While the Report was privately initiated and funded, its undertaking was urged by housing activists in Congress.)

Most of the literature on housing is not addressed to a general audience, but articles on aspects of current housing problems appear frequently in news and business periodicals. For example:

"Affording the unaffordable." *U.S. News & World Report*, September 19, 1988.
"No vacancy: the housing squeeze gets worse." *Time*, April 11, 1988.
Dentzer, Susan, et al. "A New Squeeze on Housing." *Newsweek*, August 10, 1987.

Eisenberg, Richard. "The New Vise on the Middle Class." *Money,* September 1987.

Garland, Susan B. "Teaming Up to Solve the Low-Income Housing Puzzle." *Business Week,* April 25, 1988.

de Courcy Hinds, Michael. "Owning a Home Recedes As an Achievable Dream." *The New York Times Magazine,* September 13, 1987.

Kuttner, Robert. "A Blueprint for Affordable Housing." *Business Week,* August 31, 1987.

INDEX

Page numbers in *italics* refer to illustrations.

Abandoned buildings, 28, 53–54, 126
Affordability index, 78–79
Armstrong, Robert, 42–43
Arson, 28–29
Athens, 119–21
Atlanta, 34–35

Baby-boom generation, 61, 76–77, 80, 83
Baby-bust generation, 83
Baltic Inn (San Diego), 119
Baltimore, 122
Bankhead Courts (Atlanta), 34–35
Block Grants, 128
Boston, 18, 55, 122–23
Brooke Amendment (1969), 35
"Builders' remedy," 93–94
Business programs, 96–98, 126–27

California, inclusionary zoning in, 96

Census Bureau, U.S., 15–16, 23, 24
Certificates of Family Participation, 50–52, 53–58, 109
Chicago, 18, 35, *36, 57,* 108–9
Children, discrimination against families with, 109–11
Churches, housing initiatives of, 117–18
Cities, housing initiatives of, 119–23
Cochran Gardens (St. Louis), 42
Committee for Creative Non-Violence, 15
Community Development Block Grant program, 128
Community Reinvestment Act (1977), 108
Condo conversions, 62, 65, 66, 67
Congregate housing, 119
Congress, U.S., 35, 47, 48, 55, 56, 58, 75, 83, 109
Connecticut, inclusionary zoning in, 98
Co-op conversions, 62, 65, 66, 67, 127

Council on Affordable Housing, 93, 94
Cuomo, Mario, 20

Density regulations, 92, 93
Depression, Great, 73
Disabled persons, 111
Discrimination, 20, 101–11
  against families with children, 109–11
  income, 91–96, 98
  race, 98, 101–9
Doubling up, 18–19, 38
Down payments, 74–75, 77, 81, 84, 95, 117
Driscoll, Sister Connie, 18
Drugs, 16, 38–40, 39

Elderly, 28, 65, 119
Entitlement programs, 56
Evictions, 18, 40, 43, 65
Exclusionary zoning, 91–96

Fair Housing Act (N.J.) (1985), 93–94
Fair Housing Act (U.S.) (1968), 105, 111
Fair market rent, 49
Families, 23
  with children, discrimination against, 109–11
  doubling up, 19, 38
  homeless, 18
  problem, in public housing, 37–38
Fanwood, 94
Federal government:
  necessary role of, 128–30
  public housing subsidies reduced by, 40–41, 43
Federal Housing Administration (FHA), 74–75

Filtering, 26

Gautreaux, Dorothy, 109
Gentrification, 25–26, 27, 122

Homeless, 13–20, 17, 22, 67, 83
  causes of, 19–20
  number of, 15–16
  profile of, 16–18
Home ownership, 20, 71–87, 117
  affordability of, 77–79
  downward trend in, 75–77
  future prospects for, 81–84
  and help for first-time buyers, 84
  price explosion and, 80–81
  tax deductions and, 84–87
  zoning and, 91–96
Homesight project, 126–27
Homesteading programs, 123, 124
Housing Act (1937), 33
Housing Act (1949), 11
Housing and Urban Development Department, U.S. (HUD), 15, 18, 28, 48, 109, 111, 127–28
  eligibility requirements of, 24–25, 34
  public housing and, 33, 34, 38, 40, 41, 42, 105
  rent subsidies and, 49–50, 51, 52, 54, 56–58
  scandal in, 11–12, 54
  substandard housing and, 62, 63–65
Housing Help Inc., 104–5
Housing Partnership, 121–22
Houston, 78–79
Huntington, 104–5

Inclusionary zoning, 91, 96–97

Income, 76-77
  discrimination based on, 91-
    96, 98
  HUD eligibility and, 24-25,
    34
Income tax deductions, 84-87

Justice Department, U.S., 101

Kemp, Jack, 40, 54
Key money, 69

Local Initiatives Support Corp.
  (LISC), 126-27
Low-income families, 25, 34
Low-income housing, 21-29, 83
  business construction linked
    to, 96-98
  declining supply of, 23, 25-
    29
  indicators of crisis in, 19-20
  private housing industry and,
    29, 47-58

Massachusetts:
  affordability of homes in, 78
  inclusionary zoning in, 98
Median family income, 24-25, 34
Mentally ill, 16, 28
Middle class, 20, 85
Mortgages, 73-75, 81, 96, 118,
    121-22, 123
  FHA-insured, 74-75
  prepayment of, 45, 48-49
  redlining and, 106-8
  tax deduction for, 84-87
Mount Laurel, 92-96

National Association of Home
  Builders, 77
National Association of Realtors,
    78

National Coalition for the Home-
    less, 15, 19
National Housing Act (1934), 74
National Low-Income Housing
  Coalition, 19
Nehemiah Plan, 117-18
New Deal, 73
New Jersey, inclusionary zoning
  brought to, 92-96
New York City, 18-19, 27, 28,
    40, 55, 64, 67, 68-70, 78-79,
    97, 117, 121-22, 126
"No available land" excuse, 94

Omaha, 42-43

Payment standards, 52
Philadelphia, 110, 124
Poverty, 23-25
President's Commission on Housing, 11
Private housing industry, 29, 47-
    58
  mortgage prepayments and,
    45, 48-49
  Section 8 programs and, 49-
    52, 53-58, 109
  vouchers and, 52-55, 111
Property taxes, 84-87
Providence, 120
Public housing, 29, 31-43, 47,
    56, 105, 108, 109, 112, 122-
    23, 129
  critical changes in, 34-35
  decline in federal subsidies
    for, 40-41, 43
  early days of, 33-34
  as endangered species, 40-
    42
  new pressures on, 38-40
  problem people in, 37-38
  public perception of, 35-37

Public housing (*continued*)
    race discrimination and,
      101–4
    tenant management of, 42
Public housing authorities (PHAs):
    public housing and, 33, 40,
      42, 56
    rent subsidies and, 51, 52,
      53, 55

Race discrimination, 98, 101–9
    against groups of people,
      101–5, 108–9
    against individuals, 105–6
Reagan, Ronald, 52
Redlining, 106–8
Rehabilitation, 49, *120*, 125–27
    certificates or vouchers and,
      53–54
    homesteading programs and,
      123, *124*
Rent control, 65–70
    case against, 66–69
    case for, 69–70
Rent increases, 20, 45, 61–62
Rent subsidies, 49, 50–58, 129
    certificates, 50–52, 53–58,
      109
    chance element in, 55–58
    vouchers, 52–55, 111
Riverton (New York City), 97
Robert Taylor Houses (Chicago),
    35

St. Louis, 42
Sand, Leonard, 101–3, 104
San Diego, 119
San Francisco, 28, 96
Section 8:
    Existing Housing Program,
      50–52, 53–58, 109
    Moderate Rehabilitation Pro-
      gram, 54

Section 8 (*continued*)
    New Housing Program, 49–
      50
    Substantial Rehabilitation
      Program, 49–50, 54
Single-room-occupancy units
    (SROs), 28, 119
States:
    tenants' rights and, 65
    widening role for, 118–19,
      129
Stop Wasting Abandoned Prop-
    erty program, *120*
Substandard housing conditions,
    20, 62–65
Suburbs:
    low- and moderate-income
      housing in, 93, 94–96
    public housing tenants
      moved to, 108–9
Supreme Court, U.S., 103, 104,
    105
Sweat equity, 123

Tenant activism, 65
Tenements, 29, 63, *64*
"Trade-up" market, 80–81
Treasury Department, U.S., 85

Urban renewal, 26–28, 119
U.S. Conference of Mayors, 18

Vento, Bruce F., 16
Vouchers, 52–55, 111

Warehousing, 62
Washington, D.C., 126–27
Wasicsko, Nicholas C., 99, 104
Working Partners, 127–28

Yonkers, 18, 98, 99, 101–4, *102*

Zoning, 91–97, 104–5

DATE DUE